CLARENDON STUDIES IN CRIMINOLOGY

Published under the auspices of the Institute of Criminology, University of Cambridge; the Mannheim Centre, London School of Economics; and the Centre for Criminology, University of Oxford.

RECENT TITLES IN THIS SERIES:

Policing Human Rights
Martin

Normalizing Extreme Imprisonment:
The Case of Life Without Parole in California
Vannier

Respect and Criminal Justice
Watson

Neighbourhood Policing: The Rise and Fall of a Policing Model
Innes, Roberts, Lowe, Innes

Respectable Citizens – Shady Practices:
The Economic Morality of the Middle Classes
Farrall and Karstedt

Advocates of Humanity:
Human Rights NGOs in International Criminal Justice
Lohne

Intimate Crimes: Kidnapping, Trust, and Gangs in Mexico City
Ochoa

Police Community Support Officers:
Cultures and Identities within Pluralized Policing
O'Neill

Last Chance for Life: Clemency in Southeast Asian Death Penalty Cases
Pascoe

Armed Robbers

Identity and Cultural Mythscapes in the Lucky Country

Emmeline Taylor

OXFORD
UNIVERSITY PRESS

OXFORD
UNIVERSITY PRESS

Great Clarendon Street, Oxford, OX2 6DP,
United Kingdom

Oxford University Press is a department of the University of Oxford.
It furthers the University's objective of excellence in research, scholarship,
and education by publishing worldwide. Oxford is a registered trade mark of
Oxford University Press in the UK and in certain other countries

First Edition published in 2022

Impression: 1

Published in the United States of America by Oxford University Press
198 Madison Avenue, New York, NY 10016, United States of America

British Library Cataloguing in Publication Data

Data available

Library of Congress Control Number: 2021946686

ISBN 978–0–19–885513–2

DOI: 10.1093/oso/9780198855132.001.0001

Printed and bound by
CPI Group (UK) Ltd, Croydon, CR0 4YY

For Tash
(1974–2017)

General Editors Introduction

The *Clarendon Studies in Criminology* series aims to provide a forum for outstanding theoretical and empirical work in all aspects of criminology and criminal justice, broadly understood. The Editors welcome submissions from established scholars, as well as manuscripts based on excellent PhD dissertations. The Series was inaugurated in 1994, with Roger Hood as its first General Editor, following discussions between Oxford University Press and Oxford's then Centre for Criminological Research. It is edited under the auspices of three centres: The Centre for Criminology at the University of Oxford, the Institute of Criminology at the University of Cambridge, and the Mannheim Centre for Criminology at the London School of Economics. Each supplies members of the Editorial Board and, in turn, the Series General Editor or Editors.

Armed Robbers: Identity and Cultural Mythscapes in the Lucky Country is engaging and energetic. In it, Emmeline Taylor offers a glimpse into the experiences and motivations of a group of men incarcerated in Australian prisons for armed robbery. The fluid writing style and personal interventions from the start offer sometimes amusing, and other times wrenching stories of contemporary crime and punishment in Australia.

The men, who are presented with affection but without sentiment, appear to be searching not just for thrills, but also for economic security and meaning in a country that has left so many behind. First-hand accounts make concrete complex issues around identity, class, gender, and affect, while keeping the reader entertained. This is a very readable book.

While focused on a particular group of individuals, who had been convicted of a specific crime, this book also illuminates worrying aspects of contemporary imprisonment in Australia. The impact of privatization on security, but also on other fundamental aspects of a prison sentence, such as rehabilitation and training, is devastating.

As we have seen during the COVID pandemic, Australia remains on some measurements a lucky country. Yet as Taylor makes clear, this 'luck' has always come at a price for some, most notably for the indigenous population, and more recently for immigrants. In setting out these men's experiences, Taylor builds an intimate and compelling portrait not just of crime and criminal justice but of masculinity and class in twenty-first-century Australia. In so doing, she shows the great potential of theoretically informed qualitative research, and how other people's stories can move us to reassess our own. We are pleased to include it in the *Clarendon Studies in Criminology* series.

Mary Bosworth and Carolyn Hoyle
General Editors
Centre for Criminology, University of Oxford
July 2021

Acknowledgements

Huge thanks to all of my colleagues at City, University of London some of whom read, commented on, and quite rightly suggested binning draft chapters of this book. Many ideas and schemes have been hatched with them in The Peasant since relocating to London from Australia. I'm very grateful to have such kind and interesting colleagues with a shared passion for criminology, research, and the pub.

Thank you to the Profit Protection Future Forum in Australia and New Zealand for their ongoing encouragement. In particular, sincere gratitude to Ian Seed for igniting my interest in this topic, and to Mark Gentle, Juliet Woodward, and Neil Redfern for their continuing support. Thanks also to staff at Corrective Services who assisted in the early days of the project.

On a personal note, thank you to the friends and family to whom I have banged on about this book for what seems like forever. Thank you for the journey, Jeemie (let's celebrate with a château de shít).

I am very grateful to Dexter and the 42 individuals who responded to my request to interview them and provided me with such forthright and in-depth accounts of their lives, even when their tales were clearly difficult to recount and often reflected badly upon them. I learnt a lot throughout this study and I was often humbled by the honesty and willingness of the participants to share their stories with me.

And lastly, Australia, you lucky country, I miss you!

Acknowledgements

Contents

PART TWO: IDENTITY AND PERFORMANCE

PART THREE: REWARDS

PART FOUR: SUCH IS LIFE

List of Figures

List of Abbreviations

ABS	Australian Bureau of Statistics
ACT	Australian Capital Territory
Anzac	Australian and New Zealand Army Corps
bottlo	bottle shop; a liquor store
burg	burglary
bushranger	an outlaw
cockatoo	someone keeping watch (who would 'squawk' if anyone came along)
co-ie	co-accused
CSI	Correctional Services Industry
GM	General Manager
HRMU	High-Risk Management Unit
ice	methamphetamine
juvie	juvenile detention centre
MIN	Master Index Number; a six-digit code used to identify prisoners
NSW	New South Wales
PIC	prison-industrial complex
pokies	poker or gaming machines commonly found in pubs and clubs
rap sheet	Record of Arrest and Prosecution
RCT	rational choice theory
roscoe	a handgun
RSL	Returned and Services League
segro	segregation
servo	service station
shotty	shotgun
snag	sausage
spewing	either very upset and regretful or vomiting
TAB	club with an on-site betting agency
TAWOL	the Australian Way of Life
tradie	tradesperson such as a carpenter or tiler
ute	utility vehicle; a small truck with a flatbed rear

PART ONE
ENCOUNTERS

1
Introduction

I wasn't prepared for the violent recoil of the shotgun. As the projectile soared through the dank night sky, the comb of the gun smacked into my cheekbone with such force I thought it was broken. I tried not to flinch as I brought the gun back down to my side, a swirl of smoke released as I unlatched the barrel; the smell, acrid and sour, hung in the air. A sea of spent shotgun shells was scattered around my feet. I looked around. 'She did it! Mami fired a gun!' Dexter laughed as he ran over and low-fived me. He had always called me 'Mami'. When I asked him what it meant, he told me it was a traditional West African term of affection for women, derived from the mythology of Mami Wata (translated to Mother Water), a venerated female aquatic spirit often described as a mermaid-like figure. I can only presume he was being sarcastic.

As the smoke cleared, I realized I was trembling, partly from the cold, but also as my nervous energy gave way to a surge of adrenaline. It was exhilarating. The manager of the gun club, Larry, was far more sombre. Guns weren't for messing about with. He fetched another shotshell out of the XXL-sized gun jacket I was wearing—so big I couldn't reach to the bottom of the pockets—and passed it to me. I composed myself and loaded up, raised the gun, careful this time to lock my aching cheek tight against the comb as I looked down the barrel. 'PULL,' I yelled, trying to sound confident, and Larry released the clay pigeon into the air. It crossed the sky in a blink of an eye and I missed by a mile. 'You're firing too soon. Follow the target, then shoot,' Larry coached me on 'forward allowance' for my next attempts.

It took a few goes and then, boom, I hit it. The clay shattered into tiny pieces that glistened in the rain as they fell to the ground. Larry marked an 'x' on the score sheet I hadn't known he'd been using and there was a murmur from a group of men who'd come out to watch me fire my first shots. I realized that my presence in this very male-dominated arena and my willingness to give it a go garnered a fair bit of respect from the regulars.

Armed Robbers. Emmeline Taylor, Oxford University Press. © Emmeline Taylor 2022.
DOI: 10.1093/oso/9780198855132.003.0001

The very act of firing the gun challenged their preconceptions of me as simply 'a blonde chick' (as I heard one refer to me)—this was my first valuable insight into the transformative potentiality of firearms. I had expected the visceral rush of discharging a weapon, but I hadn't anticipated its more subtle ability to shift perceptions about identity. I ended up hitting 12 out of 25. Not bad, or so I thought, until Larry nonchalantly racked up 24 out of 25, appearing to not even really look.

After firing a full round of shots, I was glad to get back into the club where it was a little warmer. It was winter in Australia and, contrary to common assumptions, and what the tourist board would have you believe, it can drop below freezing in some places. It had been raining all day and there was a damp chill in the air that had soaked right through my flimsy pumps and into my bones. The 12-gauge Beretta shotgun was incredibly heavy and my face and shoulders ached. Back in the club, a brightly lit prefab building furnished with plastic tables and chairs, walls adorned with dusty trophies and rusty plaques of bygone tournaments, Dexter ordered me a coffee and I gratefully sipped the black instant from a polystyrene cup. The members of the gun club huddled around a plastic table, a small television set mounted too high on the wall screening a State of Origin[1] match that provided a focus for attention whenever the conversation dipped.

I was sitting next to Jim. He rotated a packet of Winfield cigarettes in his hands, routinely opening and closing the lid and flicking it every other turn. He seemed wary of me, nervous perhaps, but I was there with Dexter, who was well liked and respected. He'd been going to the range for several years 'to let off a few steams' and had built up the trust of the other members. Dexter and Jim were both 'tradies', Dexter a tiler and Jim a carpenter. They'd worked for the same housing developer and knew several people in common. They reeled off a list, sounding almost ritualistic: 'You seen Jonny?' 'You know Trevor moved on?' 'Hear about Steve?' As Dexter nodded slowly, quietly sucking the air between his teeth, Jim leaned into me, eyes still fixed on the televised rugby match, 'his wife found him in his car, hosepipe through the window attached to the exhaust, engine running . . .' A chill descended on the room that was nothing to do with the temperature outside. Jim told me that Steve was close to retirement and had laboured his whole life in dogged pursuit of securing the house on a 'quarter-acre block' that was so central to the Australian Dream; to have been made redundant

[1] The State of Origin is an annual Australian rugby league football match between New South Wales and Queensland.

and now unable to attain it represented a failure for Steve, tantamount to a mortal sin.

The Australian Dream had turned into a suburban nightmare for some. The assembly lines of industry didn't just construct cars and parts; they also built the identities of the men who worked on them. The decline of the largely male industrial construction and manufacturing sector had displaced established expressions of masculine identity, bringing consequences beyond the inability to acquire material goods—Steve was certainly not the only one to experience a crisis of self. Dexter and I went outside for a smoke. The rain was now pelting down hard, so we a lit a tab and headed to his ute to drive back into town. 'Wear proper shoes next time', Larry hollered after me.

I never thought I'd find myself at an out-of-town Australian gun club learning to shoot a shotgun. Somehow, having grown up in Manchester, England, I had found myself on the other side of the world, researching the underbelly of Australian criminal culture. I had been interviewing convicted armed robbers in prisons across New South Wales (NSW) and the Australian Capital Territory (ACT) for some time. A recurrent theme among the men who used firearms in their offences was the sense of power and control they experienced when 'packing heat' (carrying a gun) and even more so when firing it. I was telling my friend Dexter about how fervently the robbers would talk about the adrenaline rush that they felt when discharging a weapon. 'You should come to the club with me, Mami. Experience it for yourself.' So I did.

I had met Dexter in March 2015 on an exhaustingly hot late summer's day. Having recently moved to a new house, I had visited a local recycling centre that sold second-hand furniture otherwise destined for landfill. I'd found a solid wooden tallboy that was exactly what I wanted. I'd taken a measuring tape with me and checked the dimensions—it should just fit in the back of my car. Wheeling it over on a flatbed trolley and opening the car doors, I realized immediately that—of course—car doors don't open the full way: there was no way it would fit.

'Heh, heh, miss, what you doin'?'

I looked up to see a tradie strolling towards me, steel-toe-capped boots, clothes smattered with paint and cement, diamond stud in his ear, braided cornrows, and a big grin. Slightly embarrassed at my misjudgement, I explained my dilemma and he offered to drive the tallboy to my house in the back of his sports ute. Incredulous now, on reflection, of how trusting (or imprudent) I was, I got in my Mitsubishi Magna and drove home, watching Dexter following on behind in my rear-view mirror.

Several months later, somewhat unbelievably, a very similar thing happened. My housemate and I were buying an outdoor table and chairs for the garden from the same second-hand furniture store. We were trying to dismantle the table so that it would fit in the boot of her car when a familiar voice called over, 'that ain't ever gonna fit in there'. Dexter laughed as he headed over, reaching for a screwdriver in his tool belt. He began to detach the table legs so that it would fit in the car boot. He had helped me out twice, so I invited him over for lunch to say thank you.

Dexter had grown up in West Africa and moved to Australia when he was 16. I was making coffee in the kitchen and we were deep in conversation about what it was like being of African heritage and moving to a predominantly white area in Australia, a country notorious for a deeply entrenched racism, institutionalized in the government 'White Australia' policy, in force for much of the twentieth century.[2] I mentioned having interviewed inmates in a particular Australian prison that still subscribed to the controversial policy of 'racial clustering', whereby inmates are segregated according to their ethnicity. In the 1990s, the prison had been dubbed 'the killing fields' due to high rates of race-based violence and a spate of murders, reaching a peak of seven in just three years. Offenders would say they'd received 'a death sentence' if they learnt that's where they were destined. As a result, the segregation policy had been implemented in an attempt to assuage race-related tensions and still endured.

'Oh yeah? So why didn't you interview me?' Dexter asked.

'How do you mean?'

'If you were interviewing guys in prison, why didn't you interview me? Me and James Locky used to run the place.'

Throughout my academic career I have encountered many offenders, including rapists and murderers, but there are few times when I have been genuinely scared. This was one of them. James Locky was a notorious serious and repeat violent offender whom I had interviewed just a couple of months earlier; in fact, about the same time that I had first met Dexter. I stopped in

[2] The term 'White Australia policy' was retrospectively applied to a series of historical immigration policies that effectively prevented people of non-European descent from immigrating to Australia. The policies were progressively dismantled from 1949, but most notably from 1973 when the Whitlam Government passed laws to ensure that race would be totally disregarded in qualifying for immigration to Australia. Furthering this, in 1975, the Racial Discrimination Act made racially based selection criteria unlawful.

my tracks. I felt sharp prickles tingle the back of my neck and could tell my face was reddening. I tried to look calm and casual as I continued to make a pot of coffee. I recalled reading Richard T. Wright and Scott H. Decker's *Armed Robbers in Action*, in which they relayed an account of 'Offender No. 81', a well-connected armed robber who, when he was arrested shortly after meeting with them, became convinced they had sold him out.

My mind was racing—was this a warning? Were the two accidental meetings at the second-hand furniture warehouse actually orchestrated? Was I being followed? I was now home alone with a complete stranger sitting on my sofa, telling me that he knew one of my most dangerous interviewees from being on the inside. I carried on making the coffee and tried to shrug it off: 'I've not come across James. There are a lot of guys in there and I don't usually ask for names.' I waited for a response, barely able to look over in his direction. Incredibly, that seemed to be enough to satisfy him and I steered the conversation back to Africa as we sat and drank our coffee. My heart finally stopped pounding.

It had been a complete coincidence; no warning, no threat ever came. Dexter became a good friend and would regularly come to the university where I was working at the time and talk to my students about life and crime and prison, and he generously offered his insights throughout the study to help me to better understand prison life and criminal culture in Australia. He also continued to help me transport impulsive furniture buys.

A serendipitous study

Life's full of unexpected twists and turns. I hadn't set out to study armed robbers. Nor had I planned to spend three years negotiating access to prisons, writing to inmates, and interviewing convicted offenders about their motivations and experiences. Jacobs (2010) has described the role of serendipity in finding suitable armed robbery targets; in my case a serendipitous encounter triggered a fascination with the individuals who commit this crime.

Just as fortuity had led to a new friendship, an unexpected meeting led to the research that furnishes the pages of this book. I had been conducting research on supermarket self-service checkout theft and had been presenting some preliminary findings at a retail workshop in Melbourne, attended primarily by Loss Prevention Officers, whose job it is to strategize against theft and fraud; 'sell more, lose less' was the motto. During the mid-morning coffee break, I was approached by a Loss Prevention Manager for a large Australian retail chain: 'We've got a real problem with armed robbery', he told me, 'it's more than doubled since last year and now the WHS [Workplace Health and Safety] are on our case. We've heard you can talk to criminals?' I was surprised by this accolade, but it wasn't one that I was going to dispute. 'Of course, what do you need to know?' I asked. The Loss Prevention Manager explained that their particular retail chain was being victimized by armed robbers, and he wanted to know if there was something specifically that they were doing, or not doing, that made them more vulnerable than other stores.

The retailer offered a modest sum of money to fund the study and it began with 14 interviews with convicted armed robbers, conducted in 2013. While undertaking the interviews, I became particularly interested in the performance of armed robbery and wanted to know far more than the situational crime-prevention strategies that the initial study set out to reveal. Why was commercial robbery increasing when the financial rewards had reduced so dramatically, reaching an abysmally low average of $400 per hold-up?[3] Did Australian armed robbers take inspiration from Hollywood heist movies? Did they practise the hold-up in the mirror? What music did they listen to on the way to a job? What did they spend the money on? I was intrigued by the lives of armed robbers and what had led them into such a serious and violent crime, one which, if they were caught, would attract a hefty prison sentence, particularly since it offered such low financial reward.

Structure of the book

This book draws together a reflexive journey into understanding the sociocultural dynamics, performativity, and affect of robbery, through interviews with 42 convicted armed robbers, as well as observations of how national mythologies intertwine with criminal identity in the 'lucky

[3] A successful hold-up is no longer the lucrative endeavour it once was. Internationally, several studies have reported that the financial yields from robberies are surprisingly low (Baumeister, 2001; Katz, 1988; Matthews, 2002). Demonstrating the typically meagre rewards in Australia, in 2009 and 2010, 57 per cent of armed robberies resulted in losses of less than $500, and just 4 per cent involved losses over $10,000 (Borzycki and Fuller, 2014). Even the most profitable of recent armed robberies, on average, resulted in returns that were generally small, given the risks inherent in committing armed robbery, such as the possibility of physical harm and/or a lengthy custodial sentence.

country'.[4] Alongside the accounts of armed robbers provided in the interviews, I present ethnographic data captured as I undertook the study in six different prisons. Included in the sample were prisons that have been dubbed 'Australia's hardest prison' and 'the killing fields'. Inmates were held in facilities ranging from maximum security through to open prisons, and some individuals were interviewed while confined to the 'boneyard' (the segregation wing).

In addition, historical events and national mythscapes are interwoven to create a rich sociocultural fabric—colonial settlement, convict ancestry, gold rushes, and a sometimes ferocious hyper-masculinity born of frustration and constructed in forgotten towns. Each contributes threads that when sewn together produce a uniquely Australian cultural tapestry. For example, the mythology surrounding the gold-rush 'diggers' provides metaphoric insight into contemporary dreams of prospecting an immediate fortune, and the national eulogizing of the Ned Kelly gang affords some understanding of the uniquely anti-authoritarian spirit that characterizes Australian masculinity. Juxtaposed with Stanley Cohen's 'folk devils', such characters have paradoxically become 'folk heroes'—go-getters revered for their recalcitrance.

Just like the performance of armed robbery, writing about it was resistant to the constraints of a linear narrative structure. Things appear to unfold simultaneously; they speed up, slow down, ebb and flow with prominence and meaning. The trajectories of the participants into armed robbery were rarely straightforward. There were stories of drug abuse, violent upbringings, getting in with the wrong crowd, muddled with the seductive and enchanting appeal of violent crime, as well as, for some, an intense self-destructivism that saw them hurtle full throttle into the most precarious situations that had little chance of a successful outcome for anyone. The imposition of structure on such tangled narratives can undermine authenticity, just as post hoc rationalized accounts provided by offenders can distort motivation and experience. As the late David Matza writes in *Becoming*

[4] Australia is often affectionately referred to as the 'lucky country', encapsulating the nation's good fortune: gold rushes, economic booms, an abundance of natural resources, favourable weather, spectacular and enchanting landscapes, and relative geographical isolation that has buffered it from many international conflicts. Yet, ironically, the term, coined by Donald Horne, and the title of his 1964 book, was a scathing indictment of the nation: 'Australia is a lucky country, run by second-rate people who share its luck,' he wrote. Horne's assessment was that Australia was 'still in colonial blinkers', lacking a progressive approach to foreign policy and the economy and, as such, Australian prosperity was a result of sheer luck rather than any strategic or innovative vision.

Deviant, 'the aim of writing is to create coherence', but I was acutely aware both that 'the risk is that coherence will be imposed on an actual disorder and a forgery thus produced', and that 'no way of avoiding that risk exists since to write is to take on the task of bringing together or organising materials' (Matza, 1969: 1).

Months went by when I was unable to write anything at all because I couldn't see any logical structure—there was no clear pathway into the circuitous and complex stories. All of the themes were so intertwined and connected that to carve the book up into chapters felt too contrived. Perhaps I could do something clever and not have any chapters? Peter Carey, after all, completely abandoned the constraints of grammar in *The Kelly Gang* (it won the Booker Prize with barely an apostrophe or semi-colon in sight). But lacking flair (and a publisher), I adhered to convention and divided the text into chapters. The book thus developed in a rather discursive and extemporaneous manner before the controls of sections and chapters were imposed. I hope that the presentation of the analysis affords a degree of coherence and structure without forsaking authenticity and truth. The voices of the participants are privileged in their own accounts so as to retain as much faithfulness to their meaning as possible.

Chapter overview

Chapter 2 provides an overview of the theoretical direction of the research. It examines the fallacies of rationality that have dominated criminological explanations (and media depictions) of armed robbery, before arguing for a more sociologically rich account of motivation that acknowledges personal circumstance, cultural context and the pursuit of wrongdoing for its own sake, a phenomenon that I term 'affective transgression'.

Chapter 3 outlines the methodology and the process of identifying research participants and gaining access to Australian prisons to conduct the interviews. Six prisons were visited over the course of the study and the unique characteristics of each institution are detailed alongside ethnographic insights gained while undertaking the research. The sample of prisons was particularly interesting, being a mix of private and state-run, old and new, and open jails through to super-maximum-security facilities. The prison cultures experienced in each of these institutions are also explicated in this chapter, including gender dynamics, power plays, and the various functionalities of humour employed by prison officers and inmates.

Chapter 4 outlines three key pivotal mythscapes: Australia's convict ancestry, the nineteenth-century gold-rush 'diggers', and the 'Anzacs'. These powerful symbols of contemporary nationhood, abound with legendary characters, encapsulate the essence of 'Australianness'. The culturally distinct aspirations of 'the Australian Dream' are explored in this chapter, alongside the ways in which the frustrations of lack of opportunity and self-fulfilment translate into criminal behaviour.

Some have argued that as the Golden Era has given way to post-industrialism, a 'crisis of masculinity' (Campbell, 1993) has ensued. The stable narratives of modernity—family, identity, and belonging—have become fractured and fluid. As jobs are no longer for life, families are splintered, people become dislocated, and so, against this unstable backdrop, a project of constant reinvention emerges as a central life task. Jock Young has identified two major contradictions that underscore late modernity, creating a landscape of unease and a fertile ground for transgression. On the one hand, the ebbing away 'of social embeddedness serves to undermine ontological security' while, on the other, a simultaneous emphasis on identities, valued for their 'expressivity, excitement and immediacy', has emerged to replace the solidity of modernity (Young, 2004: 1). In this chapter, I examine how instructive narratives of masculinity forged in the industrial era have been displaced in Australia and produce a culturally distinct expression of criminality.

Chapter 5, 'Becoming an Armed Robber', focuses on the performativity and affective elements of identity transformation, explicating the ways in which offenders attempt to transform themselves, mentally and physically, into 'armed robbers' with varying degrees of success. Some young men had been exposed to violence, aggression, and criminality from a young age, whereas others were actively recruited to commit crimes by older uncles, cousins, and fathers. Several of the offenders had devised specific robbery rituals involving drugs, music, clothing, and weaponry in order to personify how they believed an armed robber should look, sound, feel, and act. Whereas most offenders seek not to be seen committing criminal acts, the modus operandi of the armed robber is one where they take centre stage, and this calls forth a certain degree of performativity. It is this dramatized display of 'doing rob', and the corporeal reactions it stimulates, that this chapter unpacks. The transformation was particularly striking for some individuals, particularly those who described themselves as being shy, weak, and physically slight. Starting from a point of timidity and depression, some drew upon various artefacts in order to affect and embody a fearless and threatening demeanour, whereas for others little performance was required.

Chapter 6, 'Doing Rob (and Getting Away with It)', focuses on the actual conduct of armed robberies. The chapter opens with an overview of how offenders choose their target and finds that while some individuals will spend months meticulously planning and observing the premises, others commit impulsive, spur-of-the-moment robberies that are high risk and low reward.

The chapter also outlines armed robbers' choice of weapon and their willingness to use physical violence, focusing on why and when. Most reported that they were reluctant to use violence, only threatening it for the purposes of 'crowd control.' Those that had been particularly violent and caused serious injury, even fatalities, often eschewed responsibility for their actions and blamed 'wannabe heroes' for *making them* commit such acts. Although there were certainly some individuals who enjoyed inflicting pain and fear on their victims, particularly as it allowed them to release their pent-up anger and frustration, most had established narratives of being honourable robbers who would only use violence as a last resort.

Chapter 7 focuses on the self-expressed motivations of armed robbery, and crime more broadly. The 'usual suspects' of fast cash and the interrelation with drugs are expounded in this chapter. Some fantasized about a lavish lifestyle—staying in hotels, driving flash cars, impressing women, frequenting casinos, and generally throwing money around with abandon—whereas others were servicing an expensive drug addiction. Irrespective of how much money was gained from a robbery or what it was spent on, there was one thing they all had in common: the proceeds would be spent almost immediately, thus necessitating the next crime.

Chapter 8, 'The Magic Carpet Ride', moves the analysis into the realm of the visceral and sensory experience of committing commercial armed robbery. Far from rational, some motivations existed on the edge of reason. Here the participants extol the excitement, adrenaline rush, and thrill experienced through this particular crime type. Their days were long, predictable, and monotonous, particularly for the men who were underemployed. Excessive alcohol use was a culturally acceptable way to pass the hours, but only served to lower already depressed states. The absence of mental stimulation propagated a thirst for hedonic pleasures satiated only by the extremes of violent criminal activity. The chapter charts the affect and emotions from pleasure to shame, ecstasy to guilt. Yet beyond the offenders who were self-medicating their depression was a cohort who sought out the affective capacities of extreme behaviour for its own sake.

Chapter 9 identifies how and why the men were caught and convicted of their crimes, before scrutinizing the prison system in Australia. In particular, the private prison estate is explored before I go on to unpack the 'prison industrial complex' (PIC). Australia currently has the highest proportion of prisoners in privately operated prisons in the world; this chapter examines how this impacts on experiences of prison, both for the individuals who participated in this study and also more broadly.

Chapter 10, 'Such Is Life: Affect, Fatalism, and Crime', is the final chapter of the book and, in drawing together the themes explicated throughout, makes the case for theoretical renewal.

2
The Edge of Reason
Affective Transgression

Criminology: aetiological crisis

At the time of conducting the research, the discipline of criminology had been undergoing an intense period of self-reflection. Two major 'aetiological crises' had shaken the core of its theoretical foundations and, simultaneously, it had taken an unfortunate 'administrative turn' that essentially marginalized the performative and contextual aspects of criminal behaviour. Major transformations in the composition, frequency, and performance of crime were occurring, yet criminologists were at a loss to explain them.

At precisely the time many scholars were predicting decreases in crime as a result of improved economic conditions, particularly between the 1960s and 1980s, the reverse occurred. 'Slums were demolished, educational standards improved, full employment advanced, and welfare spending increased: the highest affluence in the history of humanity achieved, yet crime increased' (Young, 1997: 482). Consequently, an 'aetiological crisis' (Young, 1994) ricocheted through criminological theory, leaving many established beliefs and propositions of the canon demolished in its wake. Yet, far from an anomalous rupture in otherwise predictable patterns in crime rates, a 'new aetiological crisis' (Matthews, 2016: 2) occurred when, several years later, crime rates, against all conventional wisdom, embarked on a steady and sustained decline. The Global Financial Crisis that began rippling through the global economy in 2007 sparked intuitive concerns that a rapid climb in crime would follow. A United Nations report forewarned that the resultant economic stress presaged a significant increase in criminal behaviour:

Armed Robbers. Emmeline Taylor, Oxford University Press. © Emmeline Taylor 2022.
DOI: 10.1093/oso/9780198855132.003.0002

> Where the financial crisis is manifested through decreased or negative economic growth and widespread unemployment, large numbers of individuals may suffer severe, and perhaps sudden, reductions in income. This, in turn, has the potential to cause an increase in the proportion of the population with an (arguably) higher motivation to identify illicit solutions to their immediate problems. Whilst this may appear as a simple explanation for property crime, stress situations are also the cause of many violent crimes. Unemployed persons may become increasingly intolerant and aggressive, especially in their families. Violence among strangers may also increase in situations in which people do not have clear prospects for their future.
>
> **(United Nations Office on Drugs and Crime, 2008: 8)**

Indeed, the ripples of fiscal failing in tandem with post-industrialism impacted heavily on employment in many developed nations. The job market became fractured, uncertain, and precarious, and welfare continued to be dismantled in many post-industrial nations. Yet the much-augured spike in rates across many crime types did not materialize. In fact, crime overall reduced, thus leaving many criminologists scrambling to explain 'The Great Crime Decline'; the 'most important criminological phenomenon of modern times' (Farrell et al., 2014). A recent overview identified 17 different and vying explanations for the sustained reduction in crime, before largely discrediting their causal power one by one (Farrell et al., 2014).

The overall 'crime decline' narrative, however, obscures the fact that, following the 2008 financial crisis, there have been rising levels of violence and, in particular, gendered violence, in developing countries (Kilby and Ray, 2014). The impacts of economic downturn can be simmering and diffuse; as Bourdieu (1998: 39–40) observes, 'the structural violence exerted by the financial markets, in the form of layoffs, loss of security, etc., is matched sooner or later in the form of suicides, crime and major everyday acts of violence', before bleakly avowing that 'all violence is paid for'.

This pair of 'crises' is foregrounded here to make two important points. First, the inability of criminologists to predict, nor then to explain, the sustained crime decline has been perceived as the thorn in the side of the discipline, its 'dirty little secret' (Farrell et al., 2008: 17); but rather than highlighting a failure of criminological theory, it should instead be used to illuminate a more significant point—that the search for a single comprehensive and universal explanation of crime is futile, if not absurd. Due to the complexity and heterogeneity of criminal behaviour, theoretical dexterity is required to account for variant, divergent, and multiple causes and explanations. However, it is also important to stress that, on the flipside, 'the view which argues for unconstrained theoretical pluralism is ... not defensible either' (Giddens, 2013: 57).

Accordingly, then, the analysis presented throughout this book carefully traverses a path that navigates the theoretical chasms of reductionism and determinism on the one side, and unconstrained eclecticism on the other. Reflecting the multiplicity of motivations and drivers, the armed robbers in this study had different trajectories to their offending behaviour. There were stories of violent upbringings, parental incarceration, homelessness, drug abuse, and falling in with the wrong crowd. Of course, money featured highly in self-reported reasons for committing commercial robbery, but beneath this simplistic motive lay other factors relating to self-identity, status, the evocative iconicity of robbers and, for some, an intense urge for self-destruction that saw them recklessly embark on a path of violent abandon. While there were some old-school professionals in the sample who lamented the demise of the 'art' of armed robbery, largely they were chaotic, angry, despondent men, bleakly seeking a quick hit of hope to lift them, if only temporarily, from a morass of dejection.

The second point is that the impact of the crises has been amplified by the 'administrative turn' in criminology, whereby a large number of those studying crime have never (knowingly) met with a real-life criminal and listened to their story. In fact, the offender's perspective, remarkably, has become 'the most neglected area of criminological inquiry' (Wright and Bennett, 1990: 138). It is disheartening that so many in the discipline cocoon themselves from the very subject matter on which they claim to be experts, preferring to compress the complexity of individuals and groups into reductive numbers on a computer screen. The result? A rather tepid criminology that reduces offending behaviour to binary codes in spreadsheets and databases. And, more importantly, this type of criminology often offers little to illuminate why and how crime happens in the way that it does.

In the absence of empirical research, how can we possibly begin to understand the actions of individuals who appear to relish frightening others, who can negate or postpone feelings of guilt and shame, and who appear to recklessly pursue a course of action from which few would predict a positive outcome? Thus, attempting to remedy the empirical dormancy that had beset criminological research and aiming to offer a reinvigorated and contemporary understanding of criminal motivation, I set about forming a plan to meet with convicted offenders, the results of which are recounted in the pages that follow.

Rational choice theory

The more I delved into the world of armed robbers the more I wanted to know beyond their dominant portrayal as rational actors pursuing substantial financial reward for relatively little time and effort (see Feeney and Weir, 1986; Gill, 2000; Morrison and O'Donnell, 1996). In its simplest form, rational choice theory (RCT) asserts that criminal behaviour is the outcome of 'broadly rational choices based on analyses of anticipated costs and benefits' (Cornish and Clarke, 1986: vi). In other words, the rational criminal will execute the course of action that maximizes reward while minimizing risk. Recognizing that social actors often seek to avoid costly deliberation, preferring or needing to respond swiftly and economically, the classical RCT model was later refined to account for heuristic techniques such as 'educated guesses' in decision making. Herbert A. Simon (1990) developed the concept of 'bounded rationality', or what he referred to as 'satisficing' (a portmanteau of the words 'satisfy' and 'suffice'). According to the bounded rationality model, decision making is based on imperfect or incomplete information, informed guesses, or 'good enough' strategies.

Somewhat paradoxically, RCT has survived as a 'good enough' theory, satisficing causal explanation for some elements of criminal behaviour. Its dominance has, however, directed scholarly attention to a specific aspect of criminal decision making to the exclusion of multiple other key factors and processes that fall outside the risk–reward framework. Limiting criminal behaviour to a simplistic duality of concerns—risk and reward—overlooks important phenomenological considerations that also influence the decision-making process. For example, some offenders have been found to use a self-constructed moral compass to ameliorate cognitive dissonance and dampen internal conflicts, which can result in a course of action at odds with attaining their goal (Taylor, 2014). Furthermore, embedded within the core of RCT is the implicit presumption that criminals are pursuing the same goal—typically maximizing financial reward—which was clearly not always the case for participants in the present study. In my study, I found very few offenders who reported engaging in much prior planning; those who meticulously calculated their offences, weighing up the relative risks and rewards, were a notable exception. For most, the motives for and performance of robbery appeared to exist on the edge of reason.

Affective transgression

Recent years have seen a surge of interest in affect across the social sciences, so much so that, since the mid-1990s, critical thought has arguably taken an 'affective turn'. Representing 'attempts to understand how people are moved, and what attracts them, to an emphasis on repetitions, pains and pleasures, feelings and memories' (Wetherell, 2012), affect theory has enabled scrutiny of how embodiment, feelings, and subjectivity intertwine with social actions. Despite its recent popularity, the concept of affect is somewhat slippery to grasp and its mobilization as a theoretical framework runs the risk of becoming 'very confusing' if not adequately explicated (Wetherell, 2012: 2). Nigel Thrift (2004: 59) informs us that affect 'can mean a lot of different things' and, as a result, finding consensus about what it entails is as elusive as a solid definition. In its broadest sense, affect has been described as 'the experience and dimensions of living' (Zournazi, 2003: 210) or as 'embodied meaning-making' (Wetherell, 2012: 90).

Some Freudian-inspired analyses locate affect in psychological and physiological drives such as eating, breathing, drinking, and sleeping, for example. These are instinctual human needs that can drive behaviour in order to satisfy them. They are associated with localized sensations, such as feeling hungry or tired, and the means of satisfying them are specific; only food can satisfy hunger and only sleep can satisfy tiredness. Yet some psychologists argue that this conception of affect is too limiting in that it focuses on specific stimuli and the prescribed ways of responding to them.

Liberating affect from its Freudian synonymy with drives, in *Affect Imagery Consciousness,* Silvan Tomkins (1962) distinguished between the drive system and the affect system. For Tomkins, affects, such as enjoyment, sadness, anger, and excitement possess greater motivational freedom that stem far beyond the fundamental activities required to maintain life. In contrast to drives, affects can be activated by multiple and varied stimuli, and these may vary between individuals. Furthermore, the affective states can be intensified or tempered by equally diverse events, thoughts, and environments ranging from the purely sensory to the cognitive. Affects can also spark one another; one can be 'excited by anger, disgusted by shame, or surprised by joy' (Sedgwick, 2003: 19) and, unlike drives, can be either the stimulus or the response—that is, a cause or an effect. The concept of affect is further unpacked throughout this book into *three interrelated elements: affect as emotion, affect as transcendence, and affect as transformation.*

Affect as emotion

Synonymizing affect with emotion is the most commonly deployed meaning in criminology—to the extent that the words are often used interchangeably (see, for example, de Haan and Loader, 2002; Van Gelder et al., 2014). The emotions have long been intimated in the vernacular of crime: 'revenge crime', 'crimes of passion', the 'fear of crime', and so on. Some emotions are experientially 'positive', some 'negative' (see Yar, 2009), but the relationship between them is more complicated than it might first appear. Illustrating the positive emotions elicited from transgression, Katz (1988: 52) has described the 'sneaky thrills' experienced by some offenders, as a means to understand criminal acts that have no clear material gain:

> Vandalism defaces property without satisfying a desire for acquisition. During burglaries, young people sometimes break in and exit successfully but do not try to take anything. Youthful shoplifting ... often is a solitary activity retained for private memory. 'Joyriding' captures a form of auto theft in which getting away with something in celebratory style is more important than keeping anything or getting anywhere in particular.

The analysis of positive emotions—pleasure, exhilaration, and excitement—have largely remained the purview of 'cultural criminology', whereas the negative emotions of shame and humiliation have been examined as inhibitors to crime and as an aversive emotion that needs to be managed (Braithwaite, 1989; Scheff and Retzinger, 1991). However, any examination of how criminals might court the negative emotions in order to heighten the positive ones has hitherto escaped scholarly attention. Providing for a more nuanced understanding of the role that emotions might play in offending behaviour, my study found indicators that it was precisely orchestrating passage from one state to another—fear to elation, humiliation to exaltation—that provided the most intense satisfaction among the cohort of robbers. As Lyng (1990: 860) identifies in his conceptualizing of edgework, the 'individual typically feels a significant degree of fear during the initial, anticipatory phases of the experience ... But as one moves to the final phases of the experience, fear gives way to a sense of exhilaration and omnipotence.'

This goes some way to explain why some offenders appear to place themselves in the most precarious and extreme scenarios that only serve to heighten the risk rather than mitigate it. For example, one armed robber in this study delighted in the added anxiety that committing a hold-up 'just three doors along from the police station' provided; the deeper the negative emotions that preceded a crime, the higher the positive ones that followed it. Along similar lines, Tomkins (2008: 76) asserts that 'affects may also be invested in other affects, combine with other affects, intensify or modulate them, and suppress or reduce them' and further detaches from Freudian drive-focused theorizing when he claims that 'in marked contrast to the separateness of each drive, the emotions readily enter into combinations with each other and readily control one another'.

A cocktail of emotions is experienced before, during, and after a hold-up; fear, anxiety, excitement, and adrenaline surge through the veins of the armed robber as if administered intravenously. Affective emotions resound throughout this book—the stomach-churning fear of a robber losing control, the rage directed at 'wannabe heroes', the anticipatory anxiety and accompanying adrenaline heightened by drugs and music, the elation of gaining unexpected rewards, the guilt and shame that follows the ferocity of aggression taken too far, the eruption of laughter among prison officers at the most seemingly inappropriate time, feelings of social rejection and dejection—humour and laughter, hatred and revenge reverberate across the pages. It is clear that crime has an affective quality that exists beyond any rational calculus pertaining to financial reward. In fact, as Jack Katz (1988: 312) attests, 'the closer one looks at crime ... the more vividly relevant become the moral emotions'.

The sensory stimulation provided by criminal activity is itself seductive to some, countering an otherwise mundane lifestyle characterized by the boredom of small towns and the banality of underemployment and a lack of prospects. In this vein, the offenders can be seen as 'sensation gatherers' (Bauman 1998: 83), seeking out stimuli to awaken them from the ennui and languor of everyday life. Yet it is curious that, despite the arousal of emotions being 'deeply and intimately implicated' in criminal activity, they 'remain a somewhat peripheral topic within theoretical criminology' (de Haan and Loader 2002: 243).

Affect is often interpreted as being largely synonymous with emotions and feelings, but it is also much more than this. It is important to recognize that 'the turn to affect involves more than adding emotion to the inventory of social research topics. It signifies a more extensive ontological and epistemological upheaval' (Wetherell, 2012: 2–3). According to Seigworth and Gregg (2010: 1), affect

> at its most anthropomorphic is the name we give to those forces—visceral forces beneath, alongside, or generally *other than* conscious knowing, vital forces insisting beyond emotion—that can serve to drive us toward movement, toward thought and extension, that can likewise suspend us (as if in neutral) across a barely registering accretion of force-relations.

The following two elements of what I term 'affective transgression' seek to unpack precisely these *beyond-emotion* affective qualities of armed robbery: transcendence and transformation.

Affect as transcendence

'No one has yet determined what the body can do', Spinoza (1994: 155) famously writes in the third book of *Ethics*; and indeed it has been a focus of human endeavour since antiquity to explore the capabilities of the human body. A recurrent theme among the armed robbers in this study was the way in which they believed the enactment of robbery could transcend them beyond the ordinary limitations of their ability and distort the constraints of time. To this end, there were instances in which the affective states sought through criminal activity appeared to be autotelic: that is, pursued for their own sake (auto meaning 'self' and teleos meaning 'goal'). Several of the robbers alluded to an intense sensual experience when 'in the moment'; some described it as like stepping on to a magic carpet, others talked about crossing a line, or entering a zone.

The evocative descriptions of the 'felt' dimensions of armed robbery resonate with Mihaly Csikszentmihalyi's concept of autotelism or 'flow'. Csikszentmihalyi, a psychologist, characterized the mental state of 'flow' as being when an individual becomes so focused on an activity that they enter an all-encompassing mental state in which temporal and perceptual experience is distorted. He explains:

> Concentration is so intense that there is no attention left over to think about anything irrelevant or to worry about problems. Self-consciousness disappears, and the sense of time becomes distorted. An activity that produces such experiences is so gratifying that people are willing to do it for its own sake, with little concern for what they will get out of it, even when it is difficult or dangerous.
>
> **(Csikszentmihalyi, 1990: 71).**

Csikszentmihalyi based his theorizing on observations of and interviews with artists who would become so immersed in the process of their creativity that they, at times, would disregard the basic drives of human existence such as eating and sleeping. The concept of flow has since been applied to multiple domains in which individuals such as musicians, tennis players, and racing drivers become so absorbed in the task at hand that all conscious thought floats away. For example, the Formula One driver Ayrton Senna famously described entering a trance-like state when qualifying for the Monaco Grand Prix: 'suddenly I realised that I was no longer driving the car consciously. I was driving it by a kind of instinct, only I was in a different dimension' (1988 cited in Folley, 2009: 224).

Similarly, for some in the present study, the danger and extremity of behaviour that armed robbery requires triggered a subsumption of the individual self into an all-encompassing reality in which one's senses become exaggerated. As indicated, key features of this autotelic flow experience are the distortion of time in conjunction with a sense of omnipotence and automaticity. The immersive and transcendental capacity of armed robbery, never before examined, was a recurrent theme among offenders that was consciously conjured and pursued.

Affect as transformation

The third pillar of the affective transgression concept is 'transformation'. The meaning of the verb 'affect' relates to a scenario in which an individual might use, wear, or assume something pretentiously or so as to make an impression on others. In this respect, affect is used in the analysis to explore the performativity of armed robbery. An individual may *affect* a certain persona—a fearless violent man, a psychopath, or an erratic desperate drug addict (while recognizing that in some instances little in the way of performance is required)—in order to compel victims to relinquish money and/or goods. The transformation was more pronounced for some than for others, as they attempted to transform from timid and depressive states into a hyper-masculine, daring, proficient, and violent armed robber.

The radical adjustment of character that this required for some robbers, alongside the desire to overpower any feelings of doubt, guilt, or unease with affective surges, required preparatory routines involving drugs, alcohol, music, and props. The transformative techniques and strategies were multiple and varied but the use of drugs and music were common means of arousing the desired affective state. It is well versed that music possesses an affective quality and so it is unsurprising that it also played a pivotal role in the preparatory rituals of armed robbers. In addition, affective transgression can be used to explore and understand the way in which props and artefacts are commonly used to aid the transformation into 'armed robber'—fast cars, guns, intravenous needles, balaclavas, music—influence the scene and enable the transformation of those actors within it.

3
Prison Research

Negotiating access

'You'll never get access to prisons,' a senior colleague at the Australian National University told me with a snort. But determination and a healthy dose of mulishness managed to prove him wrong. My first break came when I was granted permission to interview in a prison in the Australian Capital Territory (ACT), where I worked. I had good relationships with senior management within the Correctional Services and had completed several pieces of research for them previously. The invaluable assistance that a gatekeeper can provide in criminological research is well versed in the literature (for example, Caulfield and Hill, 2014; Pole and Lampard, 2002), and my experience was to be no different. Having approval to interview inmates in the prison from an influential and senior employee of Correctional Services paved a relatively smooth path for the first tranche of interviews, and although there were still considerable hurdles, such as satisfying the ethics committees of both the university ('you want to interview who?!') and Correctional Services, and actually identifying who was to be in my sample, I knew I was going to be able to collect some data at least. The study began in October 2013 and 14 interviews were completed at Territory Prison.

It would then take me almost a year to gain access to New South Wales (NSW) prisons. The process of applying to the NSW Correctional Services for approval was long, arduous, and opaque. I wonder, in hindsight, if this is a deliberate ploy to weed out all but the most indomitable researchers, a fate that perhaps had befallen colleagues who were resolute that I was wasting my time. Having lived in Australia for only twelve months, I had yet to have my organizational and hierarchical naivety fully challenged. There were several instances where my application had 'disappeared' or, for some reason, had not been sent to the committee for review at their quarterly meeting, but instead was lying in an in-tray waiting for me to call up—again—to check its progress. I would then have to start once more when

Armed Robbers. Emmeline Taylor, Oxford University Press. © Emmeline Taylor 2022.
DOI: 10.1093/oso/9780198855132.003.0003

given the news that there was an error in the application, such as when a page of the stapled document had apparently gone astray. Eventually I was granted access and, a few days later in the mail, I received my golden ticket: a letter signed by the Corrective Services Commissioner approving the study.

It continued to be a long and cumbersome process. Correctional Services imposed a protracted procedure for recruiting potential participants that involved letters being hand-distributed by prison officers to inmates in each prison. A reply form was included with the letter with a stamped-addressed envelope. Only once the inmates had replied would I be able to know their name and 'MIN',[1] and begin to organize the visit. The process, although correct, was less than ideal, since each step would take several weeks, if not months, and many inmates are periodically moved between jailhouses. Then, one sunny morning, quickly checking my pigeonhole before rushing to teach my Criminological Imagination class, there was a small bundle of envelopes held together with an elastic band. I recognized them immediately—I had some replies! But a sickening feeling quickly followed this elation, because there, tucked into the elastic band, was a note from Australia Post that read 'POSTAGE NOT PAID'. I soon realized my mistake. The 'prepaid' envelopes I had sent out with the reply forms were only for mail being sent *from* the university—the frank was not valid for incoming mail. I called Australia Post immediately and explained the mistake. They, unfortunately, could not guarantee that the letters would be delivered, and so I will never know how many responses were sent and not received. But even without knowing the full response rate, a surprising number of recipients returned the letters.

Of course, not all offenders want to talk to a researcher, particularly one whose initial contact has been mediated by a prison officer. One of my favourite responses, beautiful in its simplicity, was from an inmate who had taken the trouble to reply using large calligraphic capital letters impressively penned across the full length of the participant information sheet. 'BOOT OFF', it read. Less laconically, another individual, who also declined to be interviewed, wrote to me to explain that participating in an interview was at odds with his commitment to being a 'career criminal':

> Asking a career criminal for suggestions on how to prevent robbery in Australia whilst he is in prisson [*sic*] for robbery in Australia is like asking

[1] A prisoner's MIN is their six-digit Master Index Number used to identify them. The number remains the same throughout any engagement with an Australian correctional centre.

> an Aboriginal, 'How can we steal more of your land and push you further into poverty?' You should not ask such questions. For I would be cutting off my own nose to spite my face. The city I live in is the capital of armed robbery on cash in transit vans in Australia. I would like it to stay that way... Our cultures and lifestyles are a world apart. ARMED OR UNARMED ROBBERY to me is not just a crime—it is a RELIGION where I am from. Robberies and the teaching of these offences in all their variations are knowledge and skills handed down from generation to generation, much like the university you work in. The difference is you have to have the lineage or reputation to be taught these skills. Barring the 'suggestions on preventing robbery in Australia' question, I would have been happy to participate and if you still want my insites [*sic*], although I will be released you can contact me on Facebook or Skype [*contact details provided*].
>
> **(Letter dated 8 Jan. 2016, all emphases in original)**

The question referred to here was a legacy of the initial focus of the study that had aimed to follow a conventional, crime-prevention approach. Upon receiving this letter, I amended the participant information sheet that was sent to further potential interviewees. Although some topics covered in the interviews were related to desistance and pathways out of crime, the focus was certainly not on the nuts and bolts of situational crime control.

Prison characteristics

Eventually, over the course of three years, between October 2013 and October 2016, 42 interviews with incarcerated men were completed. I visited six prisons, each with a different character and status. Some prisons were old, leaky, and damp Victorian buildings with dark, echoey corridors and a musty stench of too many bodies in close confinement. Others were modern facilities, both in an architectural sense and in their ethos towards incarceration.

Territory Prison is a new-build prison, bright and light, with a notable absence of barbed wire. It was built on strong rehabilitative foundations with a focus on transitional release, therapeutic programmes for current and former drug addicts, and an impressive through-care model. More than three-quarters of eligible prisoners (77 per cent) were receiving education and training in 2017–18, compared to just 22 per cent in NSW adult prisons

(Productivity Commission, 2019). Unfortunately, the high recidivism rate for prisoners released from Territory Prison was not seen to justify its annual accolade as Australia's most expensive prison per capita.

This is a complicated issue. The jurisdiction from which its inmates were predominantly drawn boasted the lowest imprisonment rate in Australia, yet had the highest reoffending rate. Three-quarters of its prison population had previously served a custodial sentence, suggesting that its revolving door was spinning at a dizzying pace. This is not surprising, since the average sentence length was between three and six months; criminal justice literature repeatedly demonstrates that custodial sentences of less than six months usually do more harm than good and return the highest levels of reoffending. Some officers felt they were trying to undo the damage that had already been done to inmates who had served sentences in other prisons across Australia. Economies of scale, or lack thereof, were also blamed for the seemingly inflated operating costs and this led to some ruefully anticipating the expansion of the prison (a new wing had recently been announced with a capacity of over 150 beds at a cost in excess of $50 million): as the adage goes, 'if you build it they will come'. Although expansion would assist with easing the per capita expenditure, it was entirely inconsistent with the prison's commitment to decidivism and decarceration. There was clearly frustration at the senior management level and a perception that they were not being dealt a fair hand and the odds were being stacked against them.

Rural Prison is primarily a maximum-security prison located in rural Australia. The drive took my battered Mitsubishi Magna along a deserted highway etched into striking escarpments and meandering through untamed bushland. The sun cast hazy mirages on the hot asphalt ahead and my radio periodically replaced the music from local radio stations with static noise as frequencies came in and out of reach. I was reminded of just how big Australia is and doubted that the men sent to Rural Prison received many visits from their families and friends. As the years rolled on past, each one widened the chasm between the inside and outside worlds, just as the ravines scored fissures into the surrounding landscape.

Having reached the prison, the first thing I noticed as I walked towards the prison was the noise. An incessant din composed of banging, sawing, and drilling accompanied the walk along the blue lines painted on the concrete to demarcate the preferred pathway to the entrance. This was unusual, since prisons are usually quiet and sombre, at least from the outside, but Rural Prison is a large industrial complex that employs inmates in a variety of jobs, including engineering, manufacturing, and commercial laundry. The men sent there were put to work (the Australian prison industrial complex is discussed in further detail in Chapter 9) and in many ways this felt like a positive step; far too many inmates I have met have been frustrated by being locked in their cells for most of the day.[2] They lack programmes to address their issues, have access to little education, and no vocational training to provide the requisite skills for gainful employment upon release. I was intrigued to see how the Correctional Services Industry (CSI) operated in practice.

Victorian Supermax had been dubbed the 'killing fields', following a spate of murders in the 1990s. As a result, the prison subscribed to a controversial policy of 'racial clustering', whereby inmates are segregated according to their ethnicity. The strategy resulted in an additional layer of logistical planning: coordinating when inmates from the different sections could move around the prison, have yard time, eat, and so on, so that they would never cross paths. I could see how, after so long, it had become difficult to reverse the policy: the risk was deemed too high. Talking to the inmates, it was clear to me that the racial clustering policy only served to reinforce an 'us and them' mentality.

The prison was an old Victorian building that had been retrofitted over the years with new wings and modernized facilities. It was the only super-maximum-security prison in the sample and housed several notorious criminals, including serial killers, hitmen, and terrorists. Serving a sentence here was seen as a badge of honour for some inmates compared to the 'holiday camps' they claimed that other prisons represented. In the High-Risk Management Unit (HRMU), which inmates referred to as 'harm U', a radio was playing classical music as two prison guards, Ste and Dean, ran me through the who's who of Australia's most serious and violent offenders, their pictures affixed to a whiteboard with brief notes about their offences:

> He's a sex offender—likes little boys. Murdered a toddler.
>
> He hired a hitman to kill his solicitor girlfriend—set her on fire.
>
> He murdered two cousins and then went on the run for six years in the bush. They never found their bodies.
>
> He's a truck driver cum hitman. Have you seen *Underbelly*? He was in that.

[2] NSW prisons reportedly have the lowest out-of-cell hours in the country, an average of 7.8 per day (Arlington, 2017).

He's a sick one—him and his co-ies bashed that guy in the head with an axe and filmed the lot. I was nearly sick when I was told about it. This guy is crying for his life and he just filmed it. He got a big whack for that—30 years.

He hates sex offenders and Aboriginals. Now look where he is. Bad self-harmer; eats razor blades for lunch.

The scale of cruelty that the men incarcerated in the HRMU had inflicted on others, condensed to just a few blunt sentences, was enough to turn your stomach. I was feeling a little claustrophobic and so when one of the officers enthusiastically offered to take me on a tour of the cells, I accepted, mainly so that I did not have to look at the wall of infamy any longer. I wondered how the staff here were able to get through the day without being overcome by sheer despondence at the depravity enclosed in the dark Victorian walls.

Tucked away down an inconspicuous suburban side street on the outskirts of the city, *Privatefield Prison* is a maximum-security facility. It is the second-largest prison in the state and one of two private prisons in NSW. At the time the research took place, it was managed and operated by the GEO Group Australia (a subsidiary of the US-owned global group, GEO Group Inc., one of the largest private prison operators in the USA). Following a series of 'serious and systemic failings', its contract was not renewed and in April 2019, the operation of Privatefield was transferred to a joint venture between the US company Management & Training Corporation (MTC) and Australian-based Broadspectrum.

I had an uneasy feeling before I had even passed through the gates into the compound for the first time. The waiting room was loud and chaotic, the harried staff were curt but unconfident, and the security procedure seemed ad hoc and inconsistent. Once I had registered, I was given a long and convoluted set of directions to reach the wing where one of my participants was held. In all my experience of prison visits in England and Australia, this was the first and only time that I have been given essentially free rein to walk around a prison unaccompanied. Large iron doors were left unlocked, allowing me to pass through unrestricted as I tried to navigate the labyrinth of walls and corridors. The prison was severely understaffed and the officers were trying as best they could to manage its safe operation with skeleton resources. This led to some dangerous situations that are explored further in Chapter 9.

Beach Head Prison has somewhat sensationally been referred to as 'Australia's hardest prison'. Originally used as a women's prison, it now houses male and female, sentenced and unsentenced individuals in facilities ranging from minimum to maximum security. With 1,200 inmates, it was the largest prison that I visited as part of the study, and occupied an enviable position on a coastal peninsula. The interviews took place in early summer 2015 and, approaching the prison on foot on a warm and sunny morning, I looked up at the palm trees lining the outside of the perimeter fence, swaying against a deep blue sky. I reflected on what it meant to be free. I had barely slept the night before due to an unpleasant stay in an Airbnb room, and I was feeling tired and emotional. The last thing I wanted to do was enter this prison on such a beautiful day. There was something about the juxtaposition between outside/inside, light/dark, free/unfree that was giving me the impulse to turn around and leave. I wanted nothing more than to go to the beach nearby and swim in the ocean. But I forced myself to go inside.

I met with the General Manager (GM), who was curious about the study, and she gave me some background on the prison and the men I would be interviewing. She was keen to see the voice recorder I had requested to take in, and I waited anxiously while she inspected it. She dismantled and reassembled it effortlessly, removing the batteries and casing, demonstrating years of experience searching prisoners, visitors, and, no doubt, some officers. It had become apparent over the course of the study that not many researchers visited prisons.

I was handed back the digital recorder and offered the 'conference room' to conduct the interviews: a dusty, rectangular room filled by a table that could easily seat 20 people. The perimeter of the room that would be my office for the next few days was stacked with boxes of ancient-looking papers that were being stored there. Flipping through the Workers Act 'Notice of Injury' book, dated July 1993, the pages catalogued staff mishaps and accidents—strained backs, slips, and trips. These all read as very minor compared to the violence that I knew many prison officers encountered on an all-too-frequent basis.

I asked Shane, the prison officer who had been tasked with coordinating my visit, about levels of violence in the prison. He'd worked there for 34 years and was looking forward to getting 'parole' of his own. He hoped to retire to tropical North Queensland and buy a villa beside the azure waters dotted with tropical islands and the coral cays of the Great Barrier Reef. I wondered how frequently during his three decades at Beach Head Prison he would transport himself there in his mind to escape the realities of prison with which he had no doubt been confronted over the course of his career.

Shane went on to tell me about the weapons they find fashioned out of everyday objects—shivs, shanks, and slashers—made with the intention to cause the most damage in the least amount of time. Beyond the rudimentary common items such as sharpened toothbrushes, he tells me how one inmate made a 'flip knife' using three toothbrushes welded together, and another constructed a basic shotgun out of a hollow bunk bed pole, using a nail as the trigger pin.[3] In 2016, it was announced that the prison would be closed and the land sold to developers. The political sentiment behind the decision was captured in a statement issued by the Corrections Minister: 'prisoners should not have access to such prime … real estate at the expense of taxpayers'. The intention is to build a 'mega jail' to house the state's burgeoning prison population; it had already surged 16 per cent between 2015 and 2017.

Riversleigh Correctional Centre is a maximum- and minimum-security complex for men and women. It is comprised of four separate units catering for the gender and security specification of those being sent there. The interviews took place in a prefab construction that felt more like a school or university building. Inmates' artwork was displayed on the walls and, unusually, the building was carpeted. One of the staff kindly allowed me to use their office between interviews and so I took some reading with me for the long waits that inevitably arise in my schedule.

Validity of prison research

Despite Sutherland and Cressey (1970: 68) asserting that offenders 'must be studied in their everyday life outside of institutions if they are to be understood', engagement with and direct observation of armed robbery in Australia were beyond ethical and ethnographic reach. Had the study been focused on street robbers in a densely populated inner city (see Wright and Decker, 1994), things might have been different, but, as it was, commercial armed robbers in a notoriously underpopulated country are not easy to find, nor are they concentrated in any particular area. The idea of riding around picking up potential participants was simply not viable—no matter how well connected a researcher is, and even if some 'active' participants

[3] Police recorded 1,101 assaults on NSW prison premises in the twelve months to September 2016, a two-year increase of 37 per cent, while the assault rate per 1,000 prisoners increased by 25 per cent (Arlington, 2017).

were found, it would be extremely unlikely that they would entertain the concept of engaging in a research study.

For a short while, studies of armed robbers and other criminals who had used firearms in their offences utilized questionnaires self-administered by incarcerated offenders (e.g. Wright and Rossi, 1986), a bizarre approach to methodology, not least due to the fact that many prisoners are known to have extremely poor literacy skills. The notion that the complex histories, nuanced phenomenological considerations, and decision making of serious violent offenders could be captured in a Likert Scale is baffling. Against this benchmark, I was content with meeting with the offenders in prison and accepting the limitations that semi-structured interviews might present.

In contrast to Sutherland and Cressey, Copes and Hochstetler (2010) have refuted the claim that prison-based interviews are less valid or reliable than studies with offenders in the free world, arguing that there is 'no empirical evidence that active offenders reveal different aspects about their lives and crimes than do incarcerated ones' (2010: 50). A number of studies have added empirical weight to this assertion. For example, studies that have compared the findings from samples with 'free' and incarcerated offenders have revealed consistency in the information provided (Nee, 2003; Nee and Taylor, 2000). Indeed, offenders interviewed in prison might well still consider themselves to be 'active' and simply on an imposed career break—a career that they fully intend to continue upon release (as with the extract from the letter above), and numerous participants confirmed this.

The idea that an offender's intention to commit criminal acts ceases as soon as they are incarcerated holds little weight. For many, a prison sentence is simply a temporary glitch in their career—even, at times, a welcome one, providing respite from the streets, drug rehabilitation, or much needed medical or dental assistance. For example, one particularly cold winter, Kenny (age 56) reported being in agony from a rotten tooth. One evening he half-heartedly held up a service station and then sat on the pavement outside waiting for the police to arrive, having calculated that not only would he receive treatment, but he would be back in prison and with his friends in time for Christmas.

There is always the risk, irrespective of location, that asking an offender about an offence, or indeed any individual about a sequence of events, particularly over an extended period of time, will typically elicit recollections that 'make sense' in hindsight. The unreliability of eyewitness testimony points us to the phenomenon of post-hoc rationalization; but short of observing first-hand, or even participating in armed robbery, the unavoidable imposition of narrative structure upon what was in all likelihood a chaotic and disordered sequence of events will need to be tolerated.

There are also, of course, accounts that give the offender's behaviour a thick coating of exculpatory varnish. One convicted armed robber insisted that he was simply helping one of his victims back to his feet when the man banged his head hard on his hammer—twice—resulting in serious injury. But overall, and more in line with research conducted by Laurie Taylor (1985) and Dick Hobbs (1995, 2013), and the accounts of 'stick up men' by Jack Katz (1988), the offenders in this study derived a certain amount of pride, status, and even pleasure from their offences and openly admitted to them. George Orwell's acclamation springs to mind: 'an autobiography is only to be trusted when it reveals something disgraceful', since the person 'who gives a good account of himself is probably lying' (1944). And so, while some armed robbers doused their accounts with a liberal wash of justifications (some of which admittedly were understandable, albeit not condonable), others were frank about their actions, even when they did not reflect favourably upon them.

Interview approach

The study aimed to privilege the accounts and explanations offered by the robbers themselves. The interviews were semi-structured and explored a broad range of topics, including target selection, items stolen, perceived reasons for the onset of criminal behaviour, and possible avenues for desistance. Respondents were also asked to describe the most recent commercial robbery offence that they had committed, verbalizing the process from conception to spending the proceeds (if any). This revealed the peculiarities of the performance of armed robbery, including the words chosen to utter in order to take command, and the rollercoaster of emotions experienced. For the most part, interviews flowed fluidly and developed organically, covering themes in varied orders and with different depth of focus: from planning and reconnaissance to drugs and alcohol use, from choice of weapon to family background. I tried to keep the interviews informal and relaxed and in the main I think this was achieved. As Robert (51) remarked, 'It's almost like we're in a beer garden, just chatting over a few jars.'

There was the occasional request for reassurance from some that the findings would be reported anonymously, and intermittent queries along the lines of 'should I tell you that?', since I had requested that the participants did not reveal the specific details (times, locations) of offences they had committed but of which they had not been convicted. State law obligates researchers, under section 316(4) of the Crimes Act 1900 (NSW), to report any crimes an offender confesses to but has not been convicted of, should sufficient detail be provided. Failure to do so could attract up to two years in prison. While this might provide opportune access for an ethnographic study of a women's prison, I would rather not be put in that position. Some offenders would periodically test my reaction to probing suggestions that I might be an undercover police officer or member of the parole board. In these situations, reassurances would be given and rapport would need to be re-established. For example, Jack (37) was serving 8.5 years for robbery in Riversleigh Correctional Centre. We had a long discussion about the ethical parameters of the interview and what would happen with the data. I could tell that his doubts would creep back to the fore at times and so I sought to intermittently reassure him about the interview, and all of my questions being voluntary to answer, without breaking the flow of the interview:

ET: Where do you go as soon as you have done a robbery?
JACK: You're asking too much [*sic*] questions.
ET: That's my job.
JACK: You should become, like, you know, a detective or something.
ET: I would be a rubbish detective. If people don't answer my questions, I just say, 'Okay, that's fine' and we move on. I'm not here to catch you out so I would be a rubbish detective.
JACK: Yeah, yeah, I know. I understand that, yeah.
ET: After a robbery—do you go to the pub; do you go to someone's house; do you go to the park?
JACK: To the park, after doing a robbery?
ET: You would be surprised.
JACK: Um—really?
[*both laugh, and interview continues with Jack explaining that he would go home after a robbery*]

On the whole the interviewees appeared open, unreserved, and truthful. Access was not provided to detailed individual criminal records for all participants, but findings tallied with the overview of each individual given and accounts provided by Corrections staff assisting with the project. Furthermore, many of the stories provided, particularly the more high-profile robberies of banks and warehouses, could be verified through media reports of the event and/or the ensuing court trial, should there have been a prosecution. Although the voices of the robbers in this book were heard within prison walls, their accounts and recollections enable a vivid and in-depth picture to be painted of armed robbery in Australia. Incarceration is part of their story and it would be folly to isolate the experience of the robbery from the broader trajectory of these men's lives, since many had served multiple custodial sentences and, sadly for some, prison was where they felt most at home.

Thankfully all interviews were audio-recorded with the permission of the interviewee (and the prison's GM) and professionally transcribed. In addition to the interviews conducted with incarcerated armed robbers, I also spoke with countless prison officers and other prison staff, professionals visiting the prison (including counsellors, psychologists, lawyers, and teachers), and other prisoners. I observed and listened to conversations in the 'mess' and staff rooms, along the corridors, and in the waiting room. This ethnographic data is used to supplement the interviews and, I hope, to provide a richer picture of crime and prison in Australia.

Participants were asked if they would like to choose a name by which to be referred to in any publications, but, aside from one who jokingly suggested 'Brad Pitt' was a good fit (it wasn't), the majority of them stated that they were happy to use their real name or be allocated one. It was decided to draw the majority of pseudonyms from an online source of 'popular Australian names'; some names are reflective of the national heritage of the participant, using a similar process. Some interviewees were insistent that their nickname was used, and this has been honoured: CK4♫ ('seek a fortune'), who is referred to as 'CK', provides one such example. The age indicated for interviewees is the age of the individual at the time of interview.

Reflexivity and criminological research

It has been argued that the self is a 'research tool in the inquiry rather than a threat to its objectivity' (Cousin, 2013: 4–5), yet criminology has traditionally discouraged any form of 'biographical or emotional intrusion' by the researcher on the grounds that it might undermine objectivity (Jewkes, 2011: 65). Throughout this study, it was not uncommon for individuals I encountered to make unprompted comments about my age, gender, appearance, accent, nationality, and so on. Furthermore, given that the interviews all took place in prison with incarcerated men, the process managed and overseen by prison officers, complex and shifting power dynamics were threaded through all encounters. Lumsden and Winter (2014: 3) highlight the importance of recognizing

> the influence of the researcher's social background and location, including gender, race, ethnicity, social class, sexuality, embodiment and other sites and positions of power and privilege or lack thereof, on the research process, relationships with respondents and thus the interpretation and representation of the social worlds in question.

Although the tendency in criminological research has been to suppress or gloss over any suggestion that the researcher's presence might have somehow impacted on knowledge production, in the present study I seek not only to acknowledge my presence, but also to reflect upon my personal experience of the research process and the co-assembly of findings.

Gender

It will not come as any surprise that prisons are highly gendered. One of the most common responses I received when telling people that I was interviewing incarcerated armed robbers was 'oh, I bet they love that'. I would dress plainly and conservatively; smart enough to look professional, but casual enough so as not to appear like an authority figure or, worse in the eyes of the inmates, law enforcement. In one prison I was advised to wear steel-toe boots in case an inmate stamped on my feet, but trying on a second-hand pair they felt symbolic of an officer's uniform, so I took the risk and wore flat pumps.

I spoke to several female officers about their experiences of working in such a male-dominated environment. One woman told me that for years she would strap her breasts down under her uniform in an attempt to hide any overt signs of female anatomy and reported that she deliberately adopted what she described as a 'more masculine' persona, which involved joining in with the jibes and banter even when it was invariably overtly sexist, and often personally offensive. Dean, a prison officer at *Victorian Supermax*, tells me that the female officers enjoy working at the male prison because they relish the attention they get: 'You see, it's easy to be a rose in a field full of cactus,' he tells me with a wink. 'Do you know how they recruit women here?' he continues, 'They throw a hula-hoop over them. If it slides down, they're fit enough to go into the police. If they're too fat and it gets stuck, they come here.'

There were times when I certainly felt uncomfortable. In one instance, walking past the yard, accompanied by the male GM of one prison, the inmates took it in turns to jeer and gesture obscenities at me. It was difficult to drown out the shouts of the inmates and the GM was clearly embarrassed. It would have been both scary and mortifying had it happened in most other contexts, but here it just seemed absurd—a hyperbolic ritualistic display of repressed masculinity. At times, my status as a female researcher was explicitly referred to and some officers did not think it problematic to leverage it. Having received a number of declines from previously willing interviewees one morning, the officer assigned to assist me radioed through to another wing. 'Tell them we've got a leggy blonde chick wanting to talk to them', he announces, before turning to me: 'it won't work on the paedos, but it might on the others.' The problems associated with attempting to broker interview participation using such crude personal descriptions stemmed far beyond my own embarrassment and unease to issues regarding informed consent and ensuring that the respondents had experience of committing armed robberies.

Power

Prisons are not only sites of gendered interactions, they are characterized by intense power dynamics. There were numerous occasions on which I was made unwillingly complicit in these exercises of power. One such example was on an oppressively hot day in the height of summer. I was stationed at Beach Head Prison in the dusty conference room. Some of the prisoners had been working on the outskirts of the facility, fixing fences and laying turf. The complex was vast, and a truck was required to escort the men to and from the main buildings. It was decided that it would be sensible to escort two of my participants at a time so, not knowing how long each interview would last, there would always be one individual waiting when I completed an interview. While the inmates were waiting, they were held in an outdoor metal cage, about the size of a public telephone box. I'd just finished interviewing Jez and went to inform Sandra, the receptionist, that I was ready for the next participant.

'It's lunchtime now. I'm off to get some food, and you should too,' she told me.

'But what about Daniel?' I asked. 'He's been in the cage for over an hour already.'

'He's a crim,' Sandra replied flippantly, 'it doesn't matter.'

I went on to enquire as to whether Daniel would be able to have any lunch, but the same blunt reply came again: 'He's a crim. It doesn't matter.'

After lunch, when Daniel was brought into the interview room, he was clearly agitated. His agreement to voluntarily participate in the research meant that not only had he missed his lunch, but he'd been held in the cage for over two hours in sweltering heat. I felt acutely uneasy about being made complicit in such machinations of power. Unsurprisingly, it took much longer to build rapport with him than it had with some of the other interviewees.

Another inmate whose cell I visited at *Victorian Supermax* was a child sex offender. His clothes were impeccably folded and everything was placed at carefully spaced right angles. 'We move things around just to fuck with him,' the prison officer told me. The inmate in question worked in the prison library and, according to the prison officer who showed me the facility, he enjoyed ensuring the books were in their rightful place and would spend hours obsessively checking that they were immaculately straight and lined up on the shelves. The other prisoners and staff would move the books or turn them upside down before returning them to the shelf just to rile him. In the microcosm of the prison such trivial actions become amplified into huge power plays.

Hierarchies

The prison hierarchies were clearly demarcated and, spending time in carceral spaces, one quickly learns to see them. I surprised myself by how quickly I learnt to read the display of hierarchical positioning in the body language and movement of some prisoners. While at Victorian Supermax, I was sitting in a room with a window overlooking a large open-air courtyard, on to which various doors from different wings of the prison opened out. I observed as a prisoner was escorted in my direction. He shuffled along, hunched over, head down, hands firmly grasped together in front of him, a few paces behind the prison warden. I knew straightaway there was a mistake—he wasn't an armed robber. My intuition told me instantly he was a child sex offender. Dexter had told me that paedophiles were referred to as 'rock spiders' (the repulsive etymology stemming from their preference for small crevices), and, like spiders, they hid in the shadows and tried to sneak about unnoticed. They were 'fair go' for random acts of violence and abuse from other inmates. They were in the pit of the prison hierarchy and it was unusual for them not to be held in 'segro', often at their own request to protect themselves from other inmates. Their retreat further compounded the subcultural despising.

Once the inmate had been brought in and sat down, it didn't take long to confirm my hunch; there were two prisoners with the same name and the wrong one had been brought up. The vast majority of robbers I had come across had a notable demeanour and presence. They wore their physicality and aggression like body armour: hardened and impenetrable. But, as with all shields, it was there to protect a fragility lying underneath.

Practicalities of prison research

Given that prisoners are contained within a specific location for long periods of time, it can be surprisingly difficult to actually sit and talk with them. Interviews had to be scheduled to fit in with the prison day, which was heavily routinized. Typically, the hours during which I could meet with inmates were from 9:30 a.m. to 12 p.m., and 2:30 p.m. to 4 p.m. This does not leave a lot of time and, furthermore, would inevitably interrupt an interview once rapport had been established and the conversation had reached a point of relative flow.

Unsurprisingly, there would also be extended periods of waiting. Some participants would be at work far on the outskirts of the prison complex and would require transportation to get back to the main building, others would be asleep, attending a programme, high on drugs, at the gym, or in the yard. Rumours travel quickly in prisons, and on occasion there would be whispers that I was actually a police officer working undercover to gain information on unsolved crimes or that I was in cahoots with the parole board to thwart any applications for early release.

Scott (34), at Victorian Supermax, told me that several of the inmates had declined the interview once I had arrived at the prison because, despite assurances about my independence from the criminal justice system and promises of confidentiality, they were concerned about the parole board accessing the data and using it against them:

SCOTT: A lot of people I know got the letters and they said, 'Ah, no way.' They said they believe that parole will try to get what you say and try to make out you're glamorizing armed robbery and use that against you, you know and they said, 'So be careful of that,' you know. I was speaking to people in the yard and they said, 'Nah.' They said, 'You're up for parole next year' and that was their worry; they said 'Don't'—'don't do it'—like, um, they said. They're paranoid, mate; a lot of people in the yards are paranoid. And they said—they said, 'Because parole will try to get anything you say and use it against you at the parole hearing.' I think that's what people were worried about. They were thinking—because parole's got access to all of our behaviours in here; anything that we do, parole's got access to our file—and they were saying—because I'm up for parole and I got the letter and they said, 'Be careful because parole will find out you're speaking about armed robbery and, if they deem that you're glorifying armed robbery, you're gone,' you know. That's what they think.

ET: Could it ever be viewed the other way: that parole would look at it and say, 'Oh, okay; here's someone who wants to make amends; they want to give back'—

SCOTT: Nah; because no one trusts parole in here, everyone's against parole, so they wouldn't think of parole doing anything good or looking favourably. Parole are out to get you.

These are valid concerns and highlight the importance of informed consent, stressing independence from any decision making about participants' cases, and the confidentiality of the information taken from the interviews.

There were times when I had driven for over four hours along empty highways to arrive at a prison only to find that it was in lockdown indefinitely. Checking into a motel, I would sit and wait, periodically calling the facility to see if I was able to attend, conscious of not wanting to pester them into withdrawing permission, but acutely aware that I was unlikely to be a priority to be informed when business as usual had resumed. Sometimes a prison would go into lockdown while I was on the inside, and similarly this would involve long waiting periods—no prisoners could be escorted to or from me, nor could I leave the premises. On the bright side, some of these incidents provided a valuable opportunity to talk with prison staff, overhear crackled radio messages, view interactions, and observe everyday prison life.

Prison emotion: humour and despair

> 'How many officers does it take to push an inmate down the stairs?' Dean asks with a wry smile. 'None. Didn't you see my report? He tripped.'

Arguing for a greater focus on the routine life of prisons, Elaine Crawley asserts that 'it is through the day-to-day performance and management of emotion that the prison itself is *accomplished*' (2004: 411, emphasis in original). She goes on to explain:

> Prisons are emotional places, but like all organizations, they have their own 'rules' about the kinds of emotions it is appropriate for prison officers to express (and indeed feel) at work. In consequence, working in prisons demands a performative attitude on the part of staff, an (often significant) engagement in emotion-work and, relatedly, the employment of various emotion-work strategies.

This was acutely apparent in the deployment of humour, seemingly at the most inappropriate moments. Much has been written about humour in the workplace (Collinson, 1988; Holmes and Marra, 2002), and especially its role in providing comic relief in particularly stressful, high risk, or tragic situations. Humour has been found to build therapeutic relationships, relieve tension, and protect dignity in palliative care (Dean and Gregory, 2005); it has an ability to relieve tensions in maximum-security forensic units (Kuhlman, 1988); and it has been found to be a coping strategy among emergency personnel dealing with sudden death and unspeakable trauma (Scott, 2007).

In criminal justice, several studies have examined the use of humour among prisoners (Laws and Crewe, 2016) and the police (Pogrebin and Poole, 1988). Pogrebin and Poole (1988) analysed the way in which humour is used strategically among police patrol officers. They identified four different types of humour and their functions within policing: jocular aggression, audience degradation, diffusion of danger/tragedy, and normative neutralization. Relatively few studies have examined the use of humour among prison staff. Nielson has described being 'astounded by the widespread use of humour' (2011: 500) that she observed while undertaking ethnographic research in a Danish prison. Similarly, Arnold (2016: 277) noted that 'humour within prisons is ubiquitous; it is central to prison life and the relationships within it yet represents a glaring omission from the sociological accounts of prison work'. It is therefore perhaps unsurprising that joking and jesting were also observable in the Australian prisons that I visited as part of this study, perhaps signifying that, despite its cultural specificities, comic relief is a universal response to a variety of social scenarios, including the extremities of violence, trauma, and even death.

The utility of humour stems far beyond generating amusement to play a complex and ambiguous role in social interactions and relationships. It is an immensely powerful tool, one that can be wielded by some, but not others, and serves to establish exclusive boundaries and hierarchies. One often-clear distinction is who is 'in' on the joke and who is not. As long ago as 1928, Dupréel termed this 'laughter of inclusion' that can be used to promote social solidarity and cohesion or what Arnold terms 'affective empathy' (2016: 278). Joking and teasing among peers can evoke camaraderie and implicit understanding. When jokes are targeted towards an outsider group, they affirm the social boundaries and moral superiority of those sharing the joke. But 'in' and 'out' groups are not always clear-cut—they are shifting and temporal depending on the group dynamics. Humour is therefore a double-edged sword, promoting cohesion and solidarity on the one hand, while creating division and exclusion on the other (Rogerson-Revell, 2007).

While waiting between interviews at Victorian Supermax Prison, an officer excitedly runs into the room. 'You wanna come and see this!' he says eagerly. I asked what was happening, feeling pleased to appear to have been accepted as one of them, and he replied, 'We've got a guy self-harming with a razor blade. Blood everywhere.' Suddenly my ears tuned in to the screaming and wailing echoing down the corridor. It's incredible how quickly your brain filters out all the shouting, banging, and screaming in the prison. 'Ohh, I'm not sure I want to see that,' I told him, and feigned being a little squeamish. I didn't want to observe the inmate self-harming and treat his trauma as a spectacle. The incident went on for some time and it dominated my thoughts on the hour-long drive home. I found myself trying to make sense of the officers' response—did they really delight in the suffering of another human being? Were they sadists, or was it more complex? The officer who had come to fetch me had over 30 years' experience in the prison and seemed to be genuinely well liked and respected by the other officers. I wondered if he had wanted me to witness the depths of despair that they are exposed to on an all too frequent basis[4] and demonstrate that

[4] A survey of Australian prisoners revealed that 31 per cent of prison entrants had received some form of medical intervention for a mental health disorder in their lifetime (Australian Institute of Health and Welfare, 2012), approximately 2.5 times higher than those in the general population.

such crises can be handled—taken in their stride—to the extent that they could be laughed about.

Arnold has found in her studies that humour is particularly prevalent in the aftermath of serious incidents, where its function as a coping mechanism is apparent. For example, she highlights how referring to a prisoner who has committed suicide by hanging as having a 'suspended sentence' is a common and 'expected' joke (Arnold, 2016: 278). Humour in this example, as morbid and inappropriate as it seems, plays a part in navigating the discomfort of prison life and as a coping strategy to manage things beyond one's control. 'Gallows humour' can be seen as attempts to transform crises or tragic situations into ones that are less threatening and thus more tolerable. Although the jokes might be morose and cynical, group members are able to laugh, thus lessening tensions and reinforcing group cohesion. In this way, it can serve to normalize and diffuse heightened situations.

Conclusion

The methodology utilized in this study involved semi-structured interviews with incarcerated offenders who had a conviction for armed robbery. While there is ongoing debate within criminology as to whether interviewing offenders in prison or the 'free world' elicits more valid and reliable data, the depth and apparent accuracy of findings achieved in this study satisfied my concerns. It was unlikely that the participants only revealed fabricated and superficial stories about their experience of armed robbery. The six prisons visited were each culturally unique, but in each there were recurrent themes along the lines of gender, power, and humour that structured the prison and all those within it.

PART TWO

IDENTITY AND PERFORMANCE

4
The Lucky Country
National Mythscapes and the Australian Dream

> All nations are shaped by their histories, their memories and their stories.
> By their triumphs, by their tragedies.
> By their myths and by their legends.
> Because together, these are the things that shape a nation's soul.
> And how a nation remembers its past animates how that same nation sees its future.
>
> **(Prime Minister Kevin Rudd, Anzac Day 2010: National Ceremony commemorative address)**

A country's prevailing culture is often perceived as something that develops organically over hundreds of years—without beginning or end, it just *is*. Yet the construction of nationhood in post-war Australia was far more deliberate and contrived. Against a backdrop of colonial settlement and the repression of indigenous culture, a political project to curate a shared vision of 'Australianness' was set in motion. It was a time when British cultural hegemony was perceived to be under threat by waves of European migrants and ongoing antagonisms with the Aboriginal population. In order to push an assimilationist agenda (in other words, the differences between various groups would be 'absorbed' into a prevailing homogenous culture) and attempt to foster a shared identity, a 'national mythscape' was developed to celebrate the cultural ancestry of a uniquely Australian way of life. In what follows, three pivotal moments are identified and outlined to explicate the process of retro-assimilation and convey how a history—both real and imagined—has seeped into contemporary understandings of what it means to be 'a true blue' Australian.

Armed Robbers. Emmeline Taylor, Oxford University Press. © Emmeline Taylor 2022.
DOI: 10.1093/oso/9780198855132.003.0004

The personified 'Australian citizen' first came to the fore in the 1950s,[1] drawing on Australia's convict ancestry, the nineteenth-century gold rushes, and the 'Anzac legend' as powerful repositories of contemporary nationhood abounding with legendary characters encapsulating the essence of Australianness. These folkloric narratives inform a certain type of Australian masculinity that celebrates anti-authority and that, when faced with lack of opportunity, can manifest in criminal behaviour. As the poet Clive Turnbull once remarked, 'we Australians have a large inheritance of rebellious blood'(1942: 3), and it is this characteristic alongside courage, mateship, and endurance that links these three mythologies of Australian masculinity.

National mythscapes: reimagining the past and constructing Australianness

Eric Hobsbawm, the eminent British historian, identifies the post-war era as a 'Golden Age' characterized by extraordinary prosperity across the advanced capitalist societies (1994). As the tide of general affluence swelled, living standards and prospects rose in tandem. Employment rates were high, jobs were secure, families and communities were stable. There appeared to be plenty to go around and an inclusionist mentality prevailed in Australia; everyone had the right to a 'fair go' and a happy-go-lucky ('she'll be right, mate') philosophy prevailed. Politically, the time was characterized by an assimilationist agenda; Europeans were encouraged to migrate to the 'Land of Plenty' to share in its prosperity and quality of life, and government policy towards indigenous populations was to try and dissolve their identity into the wider white community. The overarching view was not only that these populations *should* assimilate, but also that they *should want* to. The key to the integration plan was to ensure that there was a tangible and coherent Australian culture, thus motivating the ideological construction of 'the Australian Way of Life' (TAWOL), replete with its reimagining of a shared national history.

[1] On Australia Day (26 January) 1949, the new status of 'Australian Citizen' was created, serving to bolster a collective sense of identity.

A nation of convicts: the penal past

One could be forgiven for thinking that the current state of the British criminal justice system has reached a level of politically driven unsophistication with which history can barely compete. Yet perhaps one of the most callous criminal justice policies was the transportation of convicts, which, over the course of three hundred years, resulted in around 380,000 convicts being shipped to the distant plantations, penal settlements, and penal colonies of the British Empire (Anderson, 2016).[2] Although convicts were already being transported in the thousands, the passing of the 1718 Transportation Act formalized penal transportation as an official sanction. The policy was portrayed ambitiously as having the potential to simultaneously increase deterrence, enact mercy,[3] and augment the colonial labour force (Meyer, 2011). From the date of the Act until the American Revolution, the majority of convicts were sent to the Americas. However, following the declaration of American Independence in 1776, further transportation was not possible, and Britain looked to the Antipodes, establishing its first penal colony in Australia in Botany Bay (NSW) in 1788.

Over the course of 80 years (the last convict ship arrived in Western Australia in 1868), it is estimated that more than 160,000 convicts were transported, on board 806 ships, to the Australian colonies, according to the Australian government's overview in *Convicts and the British Colonies in Australia* (n.d.). Some retrospectively joke that Australia thus became the UK's largest prison. Indentured as labourers, the convicts were put to work according to their skills as carpenters, nurses, servants, cattlemen, shepherds, and farmers, or building public infrastructure for the newly developing settlements. Once freed, many were appointed to positions of trust and responsibility, as well as being granted land of their own to develop. The ambitious nation-building project provided tacit approval for many of the

[2] The first modern transportations were from Britain and Ireland to the Americas, including Bermuda and the Caribbean islands, where they became indentured labourers for fixed terms, often working on plantations alongside African slaves.

[3] Some have argued that transportation was introduced as a more humane penal sanction, largely replacing the death penalty. At the time, under what has since been termed the 'bloody code', over 200 offences attracted the death penalty, many of them very trivial, such as damaging orchards or gardens. However, scholars have since argued that the introduction of transportation simply 'widened the net' and more individuals found themselves being sentenced to this new punishment who otherwise might have received a lesser penalty, or indeed no punishment at all (Meyer, 2011; Rubin, 2012).

ex-convicts to go on to occupy considerable positions of power, which may well underscore the 'have a go' autonomous culture that has since persisted.

It is estimated that one in five living Australians has convict heritage. Up until the 1920s, educated Australians 'were obsessed with suppressing the convict stain' and 'covering up any convict ancestry they might have had' (Braithwaite, 1991: 100). The convicts were perceived as debauched characters and, given the prominence of the belief that crime could be hereditary, not something one would want one's ancestry to be associated with. Yet, once a source of shame, convict ancestry has since been refashioned into something to be proud of.

> Australian nationalists began to view the penal past as an era when the British ruling class unjustly persecuted noble workers and revolutionaries. Sent to Australia because of their 'struggles for freedom' or trivial offences, they had demonstrated their good character by founding a prosperous democracy.
>
> **(Williams, 2015: n.p.)**

In 1938, for the first time, Australia celebrated 150 years of European settlement enabled by the penal colonies.

In order to spin this narrative, the 'convict stain' was removed and replaced with yarns about brave rebels and hard-working visionaries, a far more honourable ancestry for a nation. There was undoubtedly some glossing over of the more unsavoury characters who formed part of the convict shipments, in order to represent them in the main as 'children of misfortune' made up of political dissenters and hapless victims of exploitation (Wood, 1922, cited in Braithwaite, 1991: 100); but it is impossible to ever know the accurate composition of serious and petty offenders. The British criminal justice 'experiment' was rewritten as a reintegrative success; it was 'the first time anyone … dared to fashion a society from all that is wicked in another' and it appeared to work (Moniteur, 1803, cited in Braithwaite, 1995: 141).

Some scholars have argued that criminal tendencies and violence are inherited like genetic 'seeds of sin' (Raine, 2013: 37). The 'natural experiment' of transportation, of a scale and duration otherwise unrivalled, debunks much of the genetic thesis, as John Braithwaite, teasingly informs:

> Built though it was on convict stock, Australia did not end up as a nation with a high crime rate. If you wanted to look for a natural experiment

> to test a genetic theory of crime causation you would look to Tasmania where in 1846 almost half the population were still criminals under sentence, and almost half of the free population were released convicts (Hughes, 1987: 551–2). Then there were the children and grandchildren of convicts or former convicts. Tasmania never enjoyed an economic boom to foster a flood of immigration, and other colonies erected barriers to former Tasmanian convicts emigrating to their shores. We can clearly see the foundations this stock laid for the dangerous criminal society Tasmania was to become in the 20th century! (Braithwaite, 1991: 101)

A century and a half after the last transportation ships landed in Australia, it is clear that the criminal gene pool from which future generations were spawned did not produce a distilled clustering of rampant criminals.

Bushrangers, outlaws, and the Australian spirit

As the majority of transported convicts were needed to build the nation, very few were actually incarcerated and so it was relatively easy for convicts to escape to the bushland surrounding the settlements. These early 'bushrangers'—escaped convicts who lived in the Australian bush and were either helped by the free settlers or stole from them—developed populist reputations for being Robin Hood-type figures. Their ethos became romanticized, lavished with folkloric reverence, and commemorated in bush songs. For example, 'Waltzing Matilda', often mistaken by foreigners for Australia's national anthem, captures this refusal to submit to any authority and has come to be a symbolic trait of the nation's population. The song tells the tale of a 'jolly swagman'—described as 'a happy hobo' by Johnny Cash—who takes a rest from his nomadic wandering to boil a pot of tea. Seeing a sheep roaming nearby, he catches it to eat. However, the sheep's owner and several mounted police pursue him for the theft. Preferring death to losing his liberty, the swagman commits suicide by jumping into a nearby billabong (waterhole):

> Up jumped the swagman and sprang into the billabong,
> You'll never catch me alive, said he,
> And his ghost may be heard as you pass by that billabong,
> You'll come a-waltzing Matilda, with me.

This 'anthem of unbelonging' (Marlborough, 2018) narrates the 'death or liberty' sentiment of the bushrangers that has become a heroic yet fatalistic trait of Australian masculinity.

One of the last bushrangers, and by far the most infamous, was Ned Kelly. Kelly's father, known as 'Red', was convicted of stealing two pigs in his home town in Ireland and was transported to Van Diemen's Land (now known as Tasmania), arriving in 1842 (Molony, 2001). Ned Kelly was later born in Victoria as the third of eight children. He was just 12 years old when his father died shortly after serving a sentence of six months with hard labour. It is reputed that the unrelenting attention from the police and his father's death had a big impact on Ned Kelly and by the age of 14 he had become an outlaw bushranger. Kelly and his associates went on to commit at least two armed bank robberies in the 1870s and were responsible for shooting dead three policeman. Yet, despite these criminal exploits, Kelly has emerged as a national folk hero, a celebrated outlaw, virtually deified as a symbol of a uniquely Australian anti-authoritarian spirit. His legend is encapsulated in idioms such as 'as game as Ned Kelly', used to describe the ultimate in courageous, noble, but also reckless, behaviour.

In many interviews in my study, the convicted men I spoke with would mention the legend of Ned Kelly. Tommy (age 24) was an interesting character. His fiery red hair and steely blue eyes divulged his Irish heritage. His friends call him 'Red', just as Ned Kelly's father had been nicknamed. I didn't mention the link, albeit tenuous, for fear that it would propel a sense of nominative determinism within him. He was already captivated by the Kelly legend and aspired to the reckless fatalism of his hero:

> I'd say I got arrested, because I was careless. The drugs, like—like, I didn't care. I knew I was on the run for one armed robbery. Like, I knew a hundred per cent that I'm getting busted for this armed robbery in Queensland and I just didn't care any more, yeah. I just thought 'fuck it, just go wild'. In my head I was fried. I was thinking I was—have you heard of Ned Kelly? Like, I was thinking in my head, like, 'I'm—like, I'm—'I'm a hero, like Ned Kelly', you know? Like, I'm thinking that I'm a hero; like, I'm a—I'm a—like, I was—I was thinking like I was a sick cunt. Like, of course, like, I'm Australian and that; I grew up, like, everyone: Ned Kelly the bushranger—you know, like—like, all Aussies, you know. People's got tattooed on 'em 'such is life', this and that. Like—I don't know—he's like, a hero to me, yeah. I did a project on him in jail.

The 'folkloric colouring' (Scott and MacFarlane, 2014) liberally applied to Kelly is, however, at odds with other accounts. For example, the contemporary *Melbourne Punch* referred to Kelly as 'a wretch without one redeeming point . . . murderer, traitor, hypocrite, liar and coward'. Whether he was villain or hero is irrelevant, since the project of retro-assimilation 'uncritically exploits the surface of the past without regard for original meanings and significance' (Haebich, 2008). Kelly has thus become fervently eulogized in national mythscapes as 'the best known Australian' and 'our only folk hero' (Turnbull, 1942), which perhaps offers some insight into a deep-rooted and distinctively Australian cultural psyche that revers valour and resistance in the face of authority.

The apotheosis of Kelly in Australian culture has been captured in numerous film, musical, artistic, and literary works. First screened in December 1906, *The Story of the Kelly Gang* is recognized as the world's first full-length feature film. Many have since followed including *The Kelly Gang* (1920), *Stringybark Massacre* (1967), and *Ned Kelly* (2003), with the bushranger played by well-known stars, from Australian actor Heath Ledger to the Rolling Stones' Mick Jagger. Sidney Nolan's Rousseau-inspired 1946–7 depictions of the Kelly Gang are widely considered one of the greatest series of Australian paintings of the twentieth century;[4] and in literature, *True History of the Kelly Gang*, a fictionalized novel (despite its title), won Australian author Peter Carey the 2001 Booker Prize and was later made into a film released in 2019.

Kelly has also been immortalized in song, including Johnny Cash's 'Ned Kelly', recorded for his album *The Man in Black* in 1971. Cash sings about the 'wild young bushranger' and somewhat romanticizes how Kelly 'loved his people and he loved his freedom. And he loved to ride the wide open land'. Deification of Kelly is particularly perceptible in the religious symbolism of Australian singer Paul Kelly's folk-ballad 'Our Sunshine':

> There came a man on a stolen horse
> And he rode right onto the page
> Burning bright but not for long
> Lit up with a holy rage
> No turning back for the child of grace
> With the blood red on his hand

[4] A painting of Ned Kelly by Nolan was sold for AU$5.4 million in 2010, the highest price ever paid for an Australian painting.

Never known to hurt a woman
He never robbed an honest man

As my interviewee Tommy notes above, such is the reverence for Ned Kelly among some Australian men, it is not uncommon to encounter people with tattoos depicting the bushranger, particularly the imagery of him wearing the self-fashioned suit of bulletproof armour worn during his final shootout with the police (see Figure 4.1).

Professor Roger Byard, a specialist forensic pathologist in Adelaide, had similarly noticed a trend for Ned Kelly tattoos among the deceased he encountered during forensic autopsy. In order to determine if there were any commonalities among these bodies, Byard analysed the autopsy files of 20 cases. He found that—although the population studied is highly selective —individuals shared more than the Kelly tattoos in common; they

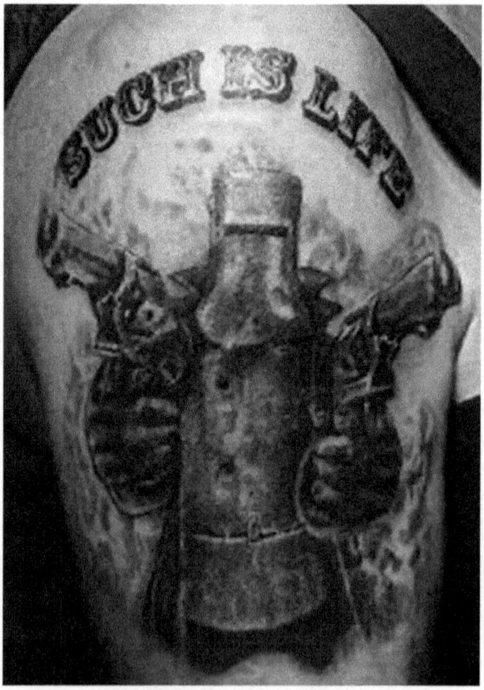

Figure 4.1 Ned Kelly tattoo depicting the homemade bulletproof armour he wore during shootouts with the police.
Source: '12 Lawless Ned Kelly tattoos', www.tattoodo.com (accessed 7 September 2021)

also had an above-average incidence of traumatic deaths and suicides (Byard, 2011: 276). He reported the following:

> All of the decedents were white males (100%) with an age range of 20–67 yrs (average 37 yrs). Seventeen of the deaths (85%) were unnatural, due to suicide in eight cases (40%), accidents in seven cases (35%) and homicide in two cases (10%). Compared to the general autopsy population suicides and homicides were 2.7 and 7.7 times higher, respectively, than would be expected, with a striking male predominance.

Byard's study sparked headlines—'Why a Ned Kelly tattoo is dangerous' (Kemp, 2011); 'Australians inked with outlaw "more likely to meet a violent death"' (MailOnline, 2011). Of course, it is not the tattoos that *cause* unnatural deaths, but they potentially symbolize a commitment to a subculture that is characterized by antisocial, risky, and oppositional behaviour that could in turn heighten one's likelihood of an unnatural end. Another study that examined the histories of individuals with visible tattoos found that there were significant links with 'childhood adversity, drug and alcohol misuse, self-harm, violent behaviour and previous imprisonment' (Birmingham et al., 1999: 687).

There has been a resurgence of Kellyana in recent years that has, in some ways, diverged from this hypermasculine adoption of his iconography to a more hipsterfied appreciation, mostly as a result of the resplendent beard and well-groomed hair that Kelly had fashioned for a photograph taken the day before his execution (as depicted in the tattoo in Figure 4.2). The 'Ned Kelly beard' became particularly fashionable in the early 2000s in Australia, and the term was even formally recognized in Australian lexicon when it was featured as 'word of the month' by Oxford Australia (2015).

'Such is life' is widely believed to be the final words uttered by the infamous outlaw Ned Kelly as he was led to the gallows on 11 November 1880, aged just 25. Although that is now contested,[5] the phrase has come to take on symbolic meaning within Australian culture, representing the plight of the underdog, the anti-authoritarian spirit, and the persistent struggles

[5] Scott and MacFarlane (2014: 731) argue that 'The footsteps and shuffling on the metal floor and the murmured prayers of Dean O'Hare, the Catholic chaplain who accompanied Kelly as he was prepared for execution, would have ensured that nothing of what Kelly may have said would have been audible to those watching from the floor below in the cavernous prison hall. The accounts published in *The Herald* that Kelly remarked "Such is life" or in *The Argus*, which reported that Kelly quipped "Ah well I suppose it has come to this" are apocryphal.'

Figure 4.2 Tattoo depicting the picture of Ned Kelly taken on the day before he was hanged at Melbourne Gaol in 1880.
Source: '12 Lawless Ned Kelly tattoos', www.tattoodo.com (accessed 7 September 2021)

of the working-class man taking on the establishment. Almost 150 years later, driving down the dusty highways that criss-cross the Lucky Country, utes and trucks roll past with the redolent 'such is life' avowal emblazoned on stylized stickers on the bumper. It is a curious statement and one that captures a unique blend of Australian masculinity based on courage, resolution, autonomy, and a certain degree of resignation and fatalism. Its criminal manifestation furnishes the pages of this book.

A rush and a push and the land is ours: panning for gold and the national psyche

Towards the end of the convict era, the discovery of gold in parts of Australia sparked a gold rush that would have a profound impact on the country's national identity. (In fact, Ned's father, Red Kelly, had found some success as a gold digger, enabling him to buy a small plot of land on which Ned had grown up.)

In 1851 five specks of gold were found in a waterhole just outside Bathurst, NSW. Edward Hargraves, originally from England, had spent two unsuccessful years prospecting in California. Upon his return to Australia in 1851, determined to make his fortune, he enlisted the help of several other fossickers and put his newly acquired panning techniques to the test. Hargraves claimed substantial financial reward from the state government and went on to name the area Ophir (after the biblical reference to a region famous for its substantial gold mines). He publicized 'his' find widely, much to the annoyance of his fellow discoverers. Just four months later, Ophir was home to over a thousand 'diggers' and the Australian gold rush had begun.

Australians and immigrants from Britain, the USA, Germany, and China flooded to the areas where gold had been found; new arrivals to the country far surpassed the number of convicts that had been sent there over the previous 70 years. Besides prospecting, the 'diggers' were unearthing an identity—and purpose—beyond British colonialism. In just 20 years the national population more than trebled: from 430,000 in 1851 to 1.7 million in 1871. Many refer to Australia as 'a nation of convicts' given its penal colony ancestry, but perhaps more accurately it is a nation of hopers and dreamers seeking swift and substantial fortune among the ribbon gums and dense bushland.

Beyond the transformative role it played, the gold rush has significance for understanding crime in Australia in a number of ways. Not least, it propelled the emergence of the first centralized police force. As the economy was booming, the population was growing at unprecedented speed and the early colonial policing, made up of a large number of disparate localized forces, could not cope with the mobility and transience that the gold rush prompted. For example, in the state of Victoria prior to 1853, the many different forces included City Police, County of Bourke Police, Geelong Police, Gold Fields Police, Water Police, the Mounted Police, and so on (Haldane, 1995). Given the movement of people, alongside the surge in population, there was a need to be able to better track offenders as they travelled interstate. In 1852 The Snodgrass Committee was established to identify the policing needs of the colony. It recognized that criminals were able to act with relative impunity when they travelled out of range of any particular division of police. This encouraged the police to centralize and acquire cross-jurisdictional powers. The Victoria Police was formally established on 8 January 1853 (Palmer, 2003).

The gold rush was, at times, a violent affair; theft, rioting, assaults, and even murder were not uncommon as thousands of people descended on the goldfields in anomic fashion; and relative lawlessness characterized the new settlements. There were ongoing clashes between the diggers and the authorities, and an intense period of civil disobedience culminated in the Eureka Rebellion in 1854.[6] The rebellion was instigated by gold miners in Ballarat, Victoria, who revolted against police corruption, exorbitant licensing fees, and the colonial authority of the British. The uprising resulted in the deaths of at least 27 people, the majority of whom were rebels, following a deadly siege by colonial forces. There was mass public support for the diggers involved in the Eureka Rebellion and this veneration of the underdog and defiance lives on in the national consciousness. In this respect, the Australian gold rush does not just represent a desire to make a quick fortune, but also holds salience for the anti-authoritarian spirit that has become etched into the Australian psyche:

> The camaraderie and 'mateship' that developed between diggers on the goldfields is still integral to how we—and others—perceive ourselves as Australians. The diggers' defiance and open disdain of authority during this time is still a dominant theme in any discussion of our history and national identity.
>
> **(http://australia.gov.au/about-australia/australian-story/austn-gold-rush)**

And so, among the forests of eucalypt and scribbly gum trees in regional NSW and Victoria, an optimistic, yet anti-authoritarian, national mentality was forged. The plight of the diggers endures in the Australian mythscape, with history lavishing only respect and admiration on the prospectors, particularly the rebels. In many ways, the folklore that now surrounds the 'diggers' is not that far removed from that of Ned Kelly—nor from the ambitions of some armed robbers, when viewed in simple terms; there is a deeply entrenched narrative that a marker of success, of masculinity and honour, is to rise above the system, seize opportunity as it presents itself, and reject the

[6] The Battle of the Eureka Stockade (1854), which gave the rebellion the name by which it is popularly known, was fought between miners and the colonial forces of Australia in Ballarat, Victoria.

constraints of authority or the convention of rules, particularly if they limit opportunities for 'a fair go'.

The Anzac legend

Into the misty Canberra dawn air, a solo bugler plays the 'Last Post' at the Australian War Memorial. The flicker of the Flame of Remembrance becomes the focal point for the congregation as the sombre sound of the lone horn is replaced by an even more resonant two-minute silence, broken only by the eerie screeches of sulphur-crested cockatoos. Every year on 25 April, the 'Anzac legend' is remembered all across Australia and marked by a public holiday in every state. The 'Anzacs' (an acronym for the Australian and New Zealand Army Corps) have emerged from Australian military history to become powerful icons of national identity, symbolizing qualities that, like those of the bushrangers and diggers, are promoted as uniquely Australian: 'mateship, larrikinism, courage, endurance and sacrifice' (Hawkins, 2013: 2). Donoghue and Tranter (2014: n.p.) argue that the Anzacs have become 'by far the most influential historical figures in relation to Australian identity' and inform a key part of the national narrative. Delivering a commemorative speech to the nation in 2010, the then Prime Minister, Kevin Rudd, roused the audience:

> For Australia, our identity has been etched deeply by what we call Anzac. For nearly a century, in fact for most of our federated history, Anzac has occupied a sacred place not far from the nation's soul. It shapes deeply our nation's memory. It shapes deeply how we see the world. A hundred years later, it shapes too what we do in the world ... So what is the story of Anzac? And how do its values speak to us today? ... Courage, sacrifice, mateship, compassion and the bonds of our common humanity. Good values. Important values. Values for a nation. (Rudd, 2010)

Stephen Garton, a historian at the University of Sydney, claims that it is not so much the Australian experience of warfare encapsulated in the Anzac legend that is unique, but rather the 'refashioning of it into a national secular religion'. Some have gone so far as to say that Anzac Day has become 'a sort of military Halloween', a 'Disneyfied' version of the horrors of war (Brown, 2014). At the same time as the Anzac legend is commemorated, the birth of the nation's spirit is celebrated. Of course, this is not unproblematic in a country still reverberating with colonial violence.

These three, almost exclusively male, groups—the convicts, the gold diggers, and the Anzacs—although historically dispersed and situationally distinct, contribute a powerful instructive narrative of masculinity and what it means to be Australian. They each epitomize the 'Aussie battler', valorized and defined as someone 'who battled on against all odds' (Macquarie Dictionary, 2012). The overarching characteristics of this constructed masculinity are determination, bold gallantry, self-belief, tenacity, improvization, and autonomy; behind the façade of the underdog, though, also lies a simmering truculence. Embedded within the mythscapes is a clear message that even in the most desperate of circumstances, one can succeed through sheer determination, if not a little brute force.

The Australian Way of Life

In addition to conveying a shared national history, identifying and articulating TAWOL came to be of central importance. White (1979) notes that references to TAWOL first emerged in the late 1940s, becoming 'endemic' by the early 1950s. So much so that in 1950 a popular newspaper columnist wrote that she was 'sick and tired of hearing people bleating about The Australian Way of Life' (cited in Haebich, 2008: 94). The government propaganda machine was clearly making an impact. The post-war Golden Years brought prosperity for many and it is during this era that the 'Australian Dream' was born.

Whereas the emphasis in the American Dream is on equality of opportunity to accumulate boundless material wealth, the Australian Dream is perhaps slightly less ostentatious: secure work, stable family, and a free-standing house built on a quarter-acre block in the suburbs, where 'snags' (sausages) sizzle on the barbie and 'cold ones' are supped with mates in the balmy summer sun. Importantly, for the Aussie battler, a key point of departure from the American Dream is that emphasis is placed more on the journey than the destination; it is as much about how one has struggled and fought on in the face of adversity as what one has achieved. Notably, few of the Australian cultural icons (including Ned Kelly and the Anzacs) enjoyed fairytale endings.

In the campaigns to encourage migration and then assimilation, TAWOL centred on this idealized lifestyle full of prosperity, sunshine, and a sense of belonging based on community and shared values. An intensive international promotional campaign was launched, driven by a 'populate or perish' mantra in the aftermath of the Second World War (Tavan, 2005). Between 1945 and 1965 more than two million migrants came to Australia with the help of generous government initiatives, such as the ten pound assisted passage scheme funded by the British and Australian governments that brought Britons known colloquially as 'ten pound poms' to the country (Hammerton and Thomson, 2005) (see Figure 4.3).

Although a large number of migrants from different countries also emigrated to Australia during this period, an explicit emphasis was placed on

Figure 4.3 A poster advertising migration to Australia.

Source: Museum of Applied Arts & Sciences, https://ma.as/52927 (accessed 7 September 2021)

the desirability of attracting the British, due to their perceived cultural affinity with Australian settlers. The presumption was that they would slot into TAWOL with greater ease. Australia had already modelled an informal 'White Australia' policy that set quotas on the European migrant intake and actively favoured migrants from Great Britain (Tavan, 2005), so when the Commonwealth Department of Immigration was established in 1945 it was not surprising that the intent to target British migrants was evident. The first Minister for Immigration declared in 1946: 'Australia hopes that for every foreign migrant there will be ten people from the United Kingdom' (Tavan, 2005).

The family was at the heart of TAWOL and viewed as the key vehicle through which to achieve a culturally homogenous nation; the suburbs became what Anna Haebich (2008) describes as the 'engines of change for assimilating one and all into a homogenous middle-class culture'. In *Spinning the Dream* (2008: 98), she writes:

> The pictorial promotional pamphlet *An Everyday Australian* produced as part of the government's assimilation propaganda, showed this new young suburban family in their brick home with its garden setting, modern furnishings and appliances and other consumer goods, including the new family car. It depicted the husband leaving for work in the city, the wife at her housework, and the family enjoying the weekend cleaning the car, picnicking with friends and playing sport. Without distinction for class, race and ethnicity this unit—male breadwinner and dependent spouse and children—represented the focus for domestic life, work, education, security, personal happiness and citizenship around the nation.

It is important to note that the symbols of Australian nationhood largely excluded 50,000 years of Indigenous Australian history. The sunny optimism portrayed jarred, unsurprisingly, with not-so-distant memories of devastating policies and practices under the assimilationist agenda. Mass land dispossession, the extensive removal of Indigenous children from their families ('the stolen generation'), forced servitude, and stolen wages were not so easy to gloss over, yet the propagandist machine moved in full throttle as if to sweep away the pain and sorrow with a cheery disposition. If the government ever managed to convince the population it had a unified culture, it was a short-lived achievement. Nearly 40 years ago, Rowse and Moran (1984: 229), rebutting the inclusiveness of Australian national identity, declared that the 'coherence that was once apparent in the "Australian Culture" has disintegrated', in part due to Indigenous peoples, women, and new migrants rejecting definitions of an Australian culture that excluded them. Furthermore, a core fallacy of the assimilationist agenda is that culture is not mutually transformative. The belief was that the cultural hegemony of the nation was so dominant that it would remain largely untouched by exposure to different and competing ways of life.

The optimism characteristic of the booming Golden Years led many to believe that growth would only ever continue. Australians were buying new homes, appliances, and cars, and the consumerist society was born. Suburban enclaves were fast developing as families flocked to the edge of nowhere to purchase their quarter-acre block—the epitome of the Australian Dream. Housebuilding and home ownership were heavily subsidized by the government in the aftermath of the Second World War. The post-war housing boom created vast and sprawling residential regions—'Melbourne with a population approximately one-eighth of London's . . . covered an area twice as large' (O'Reilly, 2012: 12)—and Australia soon emerged as 'the most suburbanised nation on earth' (Davison, 1997: 11).

As idyllic as the portrayal of the Dream was, the ideology underpinning a harmonized culture was not without problems. The aspirations it attempted to instil ignored variations in class, gender, and race, and attempted to impose homogeneity on an increasingly diverse population. It would not be long until the cracks began to appear in the heavily politicized process of nation-building in post-war Australia—particularly since embedded within the constructed Australian (masculine) national identity was a distinct and inveterate culture that reveres valour, resolution, and resistance in the face of authority.

Suburban decay, late modernity, and a crisis of identity

The transition to manhood for working-class males has for a long time been signified by the transition from school to work. In the classic text, *Learning to Labour*, Paul Willis (1977) explicates the sociocultural processes that resulted in working-class 'lads' getting working-class jobs, and how, rather than resenting the lack of social mobility the education system provided, they embraced manual labour as more affirming and authentic than other types of work. Although opportunities for progression were limited, working-class jobs, typically in manufacturing and construction industries, provided a sense of pride in the accumulation of skilled knowledge and offered stable and secure long-term employment. Anoop Nayak (2006: 814) outlines how these types of job also accrued a type of masculine 'body capital', forged 'through notions of the patriarchal "bread winner", physical "hardness" and a strict sexual division of labour that split the public "masculine" world of work from the private domestic realm of women's unpaid labour'.

As the Golden Age of suburbanization and near full employment gave way to the insecurity and precarity of late modernity, Australian working-class masculinity became strained. It was no longer possible, if it ever was, for an unlimited number of individuals to rise above the constraints of structural disadvantage, discrimination, and the intergenerational transmission of poverty through sheer hard work and determination. The cracks soon emerged, and the Australian Dream became a suburban nightmare for some. Having relocated large distances from extended family and friends, social isolation and frustration with an artificial community became the lived reality. It was soon apparent that there were tangible 'distinctions between genuine and artificial culture, mythical and actual identity, historical dreams and everyday life' (John Brack, cited in Haebich, 2008: 101). Suburban living could be monotonous, with little entertainment or social interaction to puncture the ennui of manufactured uniform living. This was the compromise made by many families seeking full employment, home ownership, and an active role in the new consumer society.

Fast-forward to the twenty-first century and Australian society has now radically changed. Home ownership has been in decline for more than 25 years as increasing house prices lock much of the population out of the market. On average, capital city house prices jumped 35 per cent in the five years between 2011 and 2016; in Sydney 60 per cent. The proportion of renters has substantially increased, bringing a transience to suburbia as people come and go, undermining the once-promised community cohesion. Post-industrialization has transformed employment, with many jobs becoming fragmented and insecure. Precarity has come to characterize the economy and 'job for life' mass employment has been replaced with temporary and zero-hour contracts, what Ulrich Beck describes as new forms of 'flexible, pluralized decentralized underemployment' (1992: 143).

The post-war period of the 1950s and 1960s, characterized by prosperity and an inclusive political outlook, was being displaced by a more exclusionary social order of late modernity in the last quarter of the twentieth century and beyond. The true-blue working-class man was under threat as jobs and opportunities became scarcer in the regional towns and cities that had previously enjoyed unbridled growth and industrial investment. In *The Vertigo of Late Modernity*, Jock Young (2007: 17) attests:

> [W]hereas the Golden Age granted social embeddedness, strong certainty of personal and social narrative, a desire to assimilate the deviant, the immigrant, the stranger, late modernity generated both economic and ontological insecurity, a discontinuity of personal and social narrative and an exclusionary tendency.

Take Geelong, Victoria as an example. Situated 75 kilometres south-west of the state capital, Melbourne, it is the second largest Victorian city, with an estimated urban population of more than 200,000. Geelong underwent substantial expansion in the post-war years, accounting for a large proportion of the state's private home development in the 1960s. Industrial growth was booming. Major employers included cement works, woollen mills, aluminium smelting, and heavy industry. But the tide started to turn in the 1970s, as many industrial businesses began to close. The withdrawal of major employers from Geelong, particularly across the traditionally male manufacturing sector, only intensified in the twenty-first century. The Royal Dutch Shell fuel corporation closed its Geelong refinery in 2014, following consecutive annual losses, and in the same year, Alcoa's aluminium smelter, based at Point Henry, was closed with the loss of approximately 1,000 jobs, as a result of no longer being viewed as competitive or financially sustainable. Not long after, in 2016, the Ford Motor Company engine plant based in Geelong closed, after announcing losses of $600 million in just five years, resulting in 600 manufacturing workers losing their jobs. Not surprisingly, unemployment rates in Geelong soared to 10.5 per cent for males and 10.4 per cent for females, while the Australian Bureau of Statistics reported that almost one in five young people (18.2 per cent) in Geelong were out of work. Tracking the increase in unemployment in post-industrializing Geelong, the crime rate had also been rising steadily every year since 2010, when 11,931 criminal incidents were recorded (5,612 per 100,000 population), reaching 18,116 in 2017 (7,400 per 100,000 population). Arguably, crime fills the void created by deindustrialization and the laying waste of jobs.

Displaced masculinities

Long stints of underemployment and the relative deprivation experienced by some of the men in this study underlie their inability to develop a sense of purpose or to carve out any significant standing among their peers or within their community. Many described growing up in the abandoned gold rush towns, in isolated and forgotten communities on the edge of nowhere, or in the decaying deindustrialized cities that had once provided stable employment. It is not surprising, then, that for men suffering from 'blocked opportunities' (Cloward and Ohlin, 1960) resulting in what Albert Cohen (1955) would describe as considerable 'status frustration', part of the appeal of robbery is the admiration and prestigious respect that cannot be accessed through legitimate means or indeed through other crime types. Economic restructuring has disrupted erstwhile processes of gender, and the masculinities forged through industrial manual labour have been 'displaced' (Nayak, 2006), leaving a gap that some fill by indulging in illicit activities and hyper-masculine criminal displays (Campbell, 1993).

Armed robbery undoubtedly possesses a level of 'criminal social capital' (Halpern, 2005: 119) which few, if any, other types of illicit behaviour can compete with. There is an enduring allure to this particular crime, stemming back to folk heroes like Ned Kelly, Jesse James, or Butch Cassidy and one only need watch any of the innumerable films depicting armed robbers as suave, honourable, brave, and intelligent men to be aware of its romanticization in popular culture. There is without doubt a certain glorified prestige that goes with armed robbery, what Hobbs (2013: 137) describes as 'a romantic aura of maverick specialism'. Illustrating the iconicity associated with it, Nick (37) described it as 'an A-class crime', 'a proper crime instead of like, you know, breaking and enters and shit like that'. Going on to explain that 'robbery puts you on a whole different scale—like the more violent the crime is the more respect you get'. The prison hierarchy was well known and observed among the inmates; 'armed robs are up there with kingpins of organizations and big drug dealers,' Kimsan (39) informed me.

Conclusion

National identity, particularly in countries still reeling from colonial violence and the dispossession of indigenous cultures, remains a highly contested concept. The construction of nationhood in post-war Australia, replete with its cultural folk heroes, produced a particular characterization of Australian identity with an emphasis on anti-authoritarianism, guile, and bravery. So synonomized have these cultural icons become that their stories are enshrined in government narratives of nationhood, passed from generation to generation, and continue to inspire countless art works, songs, and films; but clearly the construction of national values is a highly political and politicized exercise. The solid social structures that scaffolded the post-war Golden Era of modernity, such as the family and employment, have largely dissolved, rendering one's own sense of identity fluid and precarious—these are what Zygmunt Bauman calls 'liquid times' (2013). As jobs become temporary, families unstable, and communities transient, there are few anchors to which identity can be tethered, leaving a vacuum that criminal identities can readily fill.

5
Becoming an Armed Robber
Performativity and Affect

> A lot of robbers look on YouTube for videos of, like, other armed robberies
>
> **(Max, 23)**

> It's all in the way you look; the way you present yourself
>
> **(Jesse, 22)**

Despite some claims to the contrary, one is not born an armed robber, but must *become* one, however temporarily, and this involves a process of criminal transmission and a degree of performativity. How does one come to know what an armed robber says and does; how he behaves and responds in different scenarios? How does he learn to rationalize and justify his actions so as to alleviate cognitive dissonance and dampen conflict between his self-concept as a 'good bloke' and his morally reprehensible behaviours?

This chapter explicates the ways in which offenders learn to be criminal through family and acquaintances, finding that they are often enticed or coerced into acquisitive crimes and acculturated to violence by older, influential men in their lives. It then examines the rituals through which individuals transform themselves, mentally and physically, into 'armed robbers' with varying degrees of success. For some, a carefully devised routine involving drugs, music, and clothing eases the transition. In other cases, the simple script of armed robbery is idly deployed with a heavy reliance on an intimidating weapon to 'do the talking'.

Armed Robbers. Emmeline Taylor, Oxford University Press. © Emmeline Taylor 2022.
DOI: 10.1093/oso/9780198855132.003.0005

Criminal transmission: socialization and robbery

Research has highlighted the intergenerational transmission of criminal behaviour; that is, that criminal propensity can be passed on from parents to their children through learnt behaviours. It was therefore not surprising that many of the robbers in my study described growing up with male family members actively involved in serious crimes from drug dealing to domestic violence to armed robbery, and how this influenced their own criminal careers. They had been socialized to believe that violence was an acceptable means of achieving objectives such as financial gain or to elevate status. Growing up with family members who are engaged in criminal activity can influence children's propensity to commit offences themselves. It might well seem as though crime is passed through DNA, just as eye and hair colour are, but there are plausible explanations beyond genetic causality. Familiarity with those actively engaged in crime can not only normalize illicit behaviour, but also instil aspirations to follow in their footsteps. Some men described being recruited and coached by fathers, uncles, older brothers, and cousins; others talked about seeking out opportunities for an 'apprenticeship', which usually involved being the 'cockatoo' (lookout) during a job or stealing the getaway car.

Perhaps the best-known study to explore how and why crime appears to concentrate in families is the *Cambridge Study in Delinquent Development* (Farrington et al., 2009). Using a longitudinal design to follow the life course of 411 South London males from the ages of eight to 50, the study compared the conviction rates of their parents (first generation), the selected sample (second generation), and their biological children (third generation). The researchers found significant intergenerational transmission of criminal behaviour from first-generation males to second-generation males: 63 per cent of the males with convicted fathers were convicted themselves compared with 33 per cent of those with unconvicted fathers (Farrington et al., 2009). It has been argued that children can themselves become 'quasi-inmates' as they visit and communicate with parents and other relatives in prison, thus acculturating them to life inside (Shammas, 2017: 1). There are likely, too, to be many confounding psychosocial factors—structural and socioeconomic disadvantage, poor educational attainment, exposure to violence, and substance misuse among parents—that influence the transmission of crime from one generation to the next. When McCord (1991) compared the socialization practices of families where the fathers had a criminal record with those where the fathers did not, she found that convicted fathers had a greater likelihood of being alcoholic, aggressive, punitive, and absent.

Tommy was aged 24 when I met him in Beach Head Prison. He talked quickly with a nervous stutter, as he tried to say more words than would fit into the breath he had to deliver them. He had experienced a difficult childhood, and he described how witnessing his father's involvement in crime from a young age influenced his own criminal behaviour.

> Like, I, I, I grew up, you know, pretty rough and—and all that. I was living at home up 'til I was 10 and my dad went to jail for robberies and a few other things and stuff, so I went to foster care, yeah. I remember it from as far as I can remember, yeah. Me dad's always been into robberies and stuff. I seen a lot—a lot of stuff when I was younger: the police running through the house for robberies and guns and, you know, violence—violence and stuff like that. So, yeah, like, I sort of—that's all I knew sort of thing, you know? It was scary as a kid, you know. But, as I got older, yeah, I sort of wanted to be the one—like, when the family was in need or something like that—to step up while he was in jail and that, and—and—and I wanted to try and do the same thing he was doing to support us—like, what he was doing for us when I was a kid, to get money, you know?

He went on to tell me that he would repeatedly run away from the Catholic foster care home that he had been sent to when he was 10 years old. The combination of poverty, living on the street, becoming involved in drugs from a young age, a father with a history of violent offences, and a mother with a heroin addiction underscored Tommy's own involvement in crime from the age of 11.

> I spent a lot of time on the street, running away from the foster families and trying to go home, and so I was on the street at a young age, like, you know, on the run all the time from the foster family and that. And, like, growing up with me dad being an armed robber and stuff like that, I just sort of turned to it to obtain basic needs and stuff: food, clothing. When I'd go back home, you know, mum was on the heroin real bad and there was nothing at the house, you know, so I leant towards that sort of crime. It's to get money obviously. But there's a lot behind doing a robbery as well. You don't just wake up one day and go, 'I'm going to rob the shop down the road,' you know. There's a lot of things going on at home; the way you were brought up. It's about money and living—like, getting

> through life, you know. If that's all you know, well, then it's pretty hard. Growing up all these years and that's all I know . . . it's very hard to break that cycle.

As Tommy got older, he believed that prison might be a better option for him than life on the street, offering some respite, familiarity, and comfort to counter the chaos and unpredictability that had characterized his life since early childhood: 'Things were tough outside, you know, and I thought, "I'll just go and rob a few places and go back to jail. It's easier in jail. There's nothing out there. Me mum's on drugs; me dad's in jail," you know?'.

David, also incarcerated at Beach Head, had a not dissimilar story to Tommy. In 2007, at the age of 26 he had received an eight-year sentence for armed robbery. Now aged 34, he reflects back on a difficult childhood punctuated by periods of abuse, neglect, and transient care.

> Um, well, there was a lot of stuff at home, like, abuse and that, so I sort of got—I was out of home at an early age. I was taken off my mum when I was only a baby; my mum got me back when I was four. I probably stayed at home until about 11, then I lived on the streets, yeah . . . living on the streets and then the drugs—the drugs.

In the absence of a stable family environment, having lived on the streets since the age of 11, David acquainted himself with a group of other individuals who he described as becoming 'like a family'.

> So it's like—when we were kids hanging out in the city or being 13, 14, 15, you got no one to answer to and, like—and it wasn't like you're doing crime every day. Like, we'd do crime a lot, but you got a good group of mates and it was like—like a family. So you got, like, four or five blokes, you know, and you don't have to do crime all the time, because always someone's doing it and then they got money and then, a few days later, you're doing it and then you've got money; see, you help each other out. Well, that's how I was and that's how the guys I was around was, yeah. It was sort of, like, trying to live, more or less; just for living. Food and entertainment, all the stuff you do when you're a kid, but with no school, no—no parents.

At 13, David was sent to 'juvie' (juvenile detention) which set in motion his ongoing involvement with the criminal justice system.

> Um, I went to juvie because my mum called the police on me, um . . . I took money from her when I was a young teenager. Um, I think it was just a way of me getting back at her—retaliation. Um, in a weird way, I was sort of, like—'hah!'—I've turned out a lot like her, with traces of her, you know, like not really worrying about other people too much.

Having completed five years in prison for armed robbery without incident, David was granted parole to finish the remaining three years on licence in the community. He said he found the extensive parole conditions difficult to adhere to while in the community and he grew nervous of his impending independence from the criminal justice system. With just ten months left of his sentence he was involved in a fight—an act he described as 'self-sabotage'—and was swiftly returned to prison for breach of parole with a further year added to his sentence.

Liam (31) would 'rather not say' how many commercial robberies he had committed in the 19 years since his first one at the age of 12. He was taken into care as a toddler and described being exposed to criminal activity from a young age, engaging in petty crimes himself 'out of boredom', before likening his escalating criminal pursuits to building a career:

> It started off, you know, out of boredom—not going to school or anything. All day we had together as a group with nothing else to do. You know, like, when you're a teenager and you're going to school and you're chasing, you know, a career path or whatever—well—I was just in a bad—bad scene. So that was—that's what I was doing. Robbery became the path that I went down. That was my career, sort of thing.

Travis Hirschi (1969: 115–16) somewhat contemptuously asserts that 'the criminal career does not appear to be a career of increasing skill and sophistication but the reverse, a career that starts with little of either and goes downhill from there'. This conclusion has come under increasing scrutiny in recent years, particularly with regard to residential burglars. Acquisitive criminals have been found to develop 'professional' experience and a commitment to their chosen crime akin to a career (for example, see Nee and Meenaghan, 2006; Nee and Taylor, 2000; Taylor, 2017a; Wright and Decker, 1994). In the present study, some robbers (CK, for example) would refer to the money they stole as 'wages' and several alluded to the 'job'. Chris likened robbery to going to work:

> It was just like someone getting up and going to work, I guess. It was—I didn't think about it; I just did it, you know. It wasn't enjoyable; it wasn't something I didn't like either. I didn't worry about it; it was just something that needed to happen. It was just how I made money.

Despite the growing body of research that illustrates that some offenders synonymize their criminal enterprises with an occupation—and the important rehabilitation indicators that this provides (Taylor, 2017a)—no studies to date have explored whether this is the case for commercial armed robbers. There is a need for more empirical research in this area to ascertain whether robbers strive for professional status and seek recognition for their skill and expertise via criminal behaviour.

Tommy, David, and Liam's biographies exemplify how the culture within which they were living as children had a deleterious impact on their view of society and, importantly, on how to generate money to live. They were routinely exposed to violence and abuse, as well as having parental figures demonstrate that the way to get money was through criminal activity such as robbery and theft. Looking for a sense of belonging, peers and associates replaced absent familial care. Theories such as Sutherland's (1947) Differential Association illustrate how delinquents often begin their criminal careers through contact with pro-criminal companions which serves to promote the transmission of values that are favourable to violation of the law.[1] Many offenders describe how friendships were forged with criminal associates from an early age and how this provided an environment conducive to motivating, justifying, and even enjoying the camaraderie that criminal activities provided. Participants in my study had similar stories, their accounts relayed in the chapters that follow, but while many had been passively socialized into crime through their ongoing exposure to it, others, such as Sammy, were actively recruited by family members to take part in their criminal enterprises.

[1] Learning to be a criminal, according to Sutherland, is comprised of two sets of elements. One set encompasses the techniques and skills required to commit a crime. These might be fairly obvious, common-sense methods that most members of a society could have a reasonable chance of knowing (how to snatch a handbag when the owner is not looking, for example), or they might be highly specialized skills that only certain experts possess (how to hotwire a car). The second set of learnt behaviours relate to the vocabularies of crime: the motives, rationalizations, and attitudes that offenders deploy in order to engage in otherwise immoral activities.

Learning the ropes: active recruitment to a life of crime

Sammy was just 12 years old when he carried out his first hold-up. Having chosen the target, an out-of-town betting shop, his uncle and older acquaintances planned how they would go about committing the robbery. Sammy was delegated the task of 'crowd control' and, being the smallest of the group, would need to jump up on to the counter in order to take command: 'because I was so young, I had to jump the counter and twist my body to fit through the Perspex and get over the other side,' he explained. The robbery gang constructed a makeshift booth from piled-up cardboard boxes in the garage beside the house and 'set up a few mattresses' to break the fall. Each day Sammy would practise the jump, clipping his feet on the boxes, sending them, and him, crashing to the floor. He worked hard at it, eager to please his older companions and, following two weeks of practice, he was proficient at clearing the boxes. He knew the time had come.

Storming into the bookmakers the next day with a .22 pump-action rifle, Sammy made the jump. High up on the counter, his hands shaking violently, he shouted the words he'd practised alone in the mirror, 'Fill the bags up,' trying hard to bridle the quiver in his voice. The stunned manager was 'in shock and looked like he couldn't believe what had just happened'. He was motionless, and, according to Sammy, pretending that the safe was inaccessible behind a locked door. Sammy, now 31, recollects how he escalated duress, knowing that the success of the robbery, and perhaps more importantly, his status and reputation among his acquaintances, hinged upon coercing the manager to follow his instructions.

> I turned to [the manager] and said, 'Open the safe,' you know, like very dramatically, and I was shaking; you know, I was petrified ... The boys told me if they're not doing what you say, just let one off, 'BANG', and see where it goes from there ... If he doesn't do it, then hit him, you know. And, if he still doesn't do it, hit him with the gun, you know, and shoot him in the foot, you know, or—whatever, you know; like just try and get as much money as you can before you shit yourself and have to leg it, you know? The manager looked up, looked at the door, [*gestured*] that the door was locked, and that's when I just went 'BOOM' [*discharged the firearm at the manager's feet*] and yeah, then he went to the safe because

> the safe was behind the counter, not in a separate room or anything. And yeah, he just knelt down and filled the bag up.

The fear subsided, giving way to exhilaration, as Sammy realized that the robbery had been a success:

> I felt awesome, you know? I think at that—like, in that instant, I sort of felt in control, powerful. But, you know, now, when I think about it, I was very scared at the same time. I . . . had something to prove.

Sammy went on to commit a further two armed robberies, but was eventually caught and convicted of all three, and was serving 5.5 years in custody at the time of interview.

Like Sammy, many of the men in this study talked about how they admired their father or older brothers, uncles, and cousins who were involved in crime because of the power, status, and control it afforded them. In most other contexts Sammy's uncle would be considered an avuncular and nurturing influence, but as it was, he was schooling a 12-year-old child in the use of firearms for his own financial gain. Aside from the potential pecuniary reward and the prospect of pleasing his uncle, Sammy's story reveals something hugely significant about the experiential aspects of armed robbery: that is, the cocktail of emotions beyond the anticipation of monetary reward that can be experienced before, during, and after armed robbery. Fear, anxiety, excitement, and adrenaline surge through the armed robber as if administered intravenously. This embodied visceral response to committing serious violent crime is important for understanding the complexity of offender motivation.

Performativity and transformation: embodying an armed robber

'It was just something to do,' Billy, a 20-year-old crack and speed user, told me with a shrug when I asked him what motivated him to commit robberies 'at least once a week' until being jailed for aggravated robbery. His detached and simple answer was in keeping with his demeanour—he was shy and awkward and sat chewing his way through the cuff on his prison-issued tracksuit sleeve as we talked about his experiences as an armed robber. 'I guess it makes you *feel*,' he continued, 'it makes you *feel alive*; it makes you feel better about yourself . . . more—more in control; more confident.'

Before interviewing Billy, I had been given a run-down of his rap sheet.[2] In his 20 short years he'd done some pretty nasty stuff and appeared to delight in the instrumentality of unprovoked violence. I was steeling myself for an intimidating and difficult encounter. Having braced myself, I opened the door to the prison interview room and confidently announced who I was. Fully prepared for a hostile response, I was shocked by what I found. There, cowering in the corner, cradling himself and barely able to look at me, sat the same man who'd been storming into shops, service stations, and fast-food outlets, brutally attacking employees with machetes and sawn-off shotguns, since the age of 16. I could not reconcile the two Billys. I softened my demeanour and sat down.

This was the first time I really began to understand the multiple complexities of 'doing rob', and particularly its emotional, transformative, and identity-building capacities. There was clearly something driving Billy's offences beyond the desire for quick cash and the need to fund a drug habit; self-medicating his depression was his self-assessed aetiology. Indeed, several studies have found that offenders use violent crime as a means of improving their self-esteem (Athens, 1989; Gilligan, 2000; Jackson-Jacobs, 2013; Luckenbill, 1977). Through the pursuit of armed robbery, Billy was able to transcend his usual self to embody an identity he revered—hyper-masculine, capable, fearless, and proficient—thus asserting control, if only momentarily, over a life he felt was otherwise stagnating. Perhaps there are, as Jack Katz (1988: 3) claims, some 'distinctive attractions of robbery' beyond financial reward that are not attainable through other crime types.

As with most law-breaking categories, the performance of robbery is certainly not uniform; street robbers are different from bank robbers, those who use AK47s to instil fear and compliance are different from those who use a 'fit' (syringe); some robbers like to get wired before a job, others insist on the clarity and precision only attained through sobriety; some robbers scream and shout while others prefer the intense warped intimacy of a violent instruction whispered into an unsuspecting ear. Even 'offending behaviours that are topographically identical may be functionally dissimilar' (Howells et al., 2004: 179) and as with other categories of offenders, the construction of a morally acceptable modus operandi varies between robbers. Just as considerable variance exists in the performance of armed robbery, its motivations, drivers, and anticipated rewards are similarly heterogeneous.

[2] Originating in the USA as an abbreviation of the FBI's 'Record of Arrest and Prosecution' sheet, a 'rap sheet' is a colloquialism used to describe someone's criminal record.

Multiple symbolic artefacts are drawn upon as shorthand signifiers for robbery: balaclavas, dark clothing, brandishing weapons such as knives and guns, and affecting a certain demeanour. In this respect, even in the absence of planning, amateur excursions into robbery can have some success by drawing on its symbolic violence and scripted performance. As Nassauer (2018: 125) notes:

> Even if a clerk has never been in a robbery, she or he knows to be in one when a perpetrator enters with gun in hand. This ritual is understood universally, and clear rules exist in people's minds regarding what needs to be done and how to behave.

Cameron (27) explained that so universal are the symbolic mechanisms of robbery that no words need be uttered unless, of course, the victim offers up any resistance:

> When you show a weapon you don't need to say anything; you don't need to threaten them because *that* is the threatening gesture. Who's going to walk into a business with a weapon unless they intend to rob it? If they've seen the weapon and they still don't want to give it up, then I guess you verbally threaten them, but that has never happened to me.

Similarly, Murray (32) described the process as 'pretty simple' when the correct signifiers of robbery are deployed, summing up a robbery of a pharmacy: 'I had a stocking over my face. I just showed them my knife and said, "put the money in the bag," and they did'. However, despite the simplicity of robbery, offenders still need to get into character. Some participants described a carefully devised robbery routine involving drugs, music, and clothing to orchestrate their transition and enable an otherwise anxious, desolate, and hesitant individual to embody the persona of a confident and competent armed robber. Their methods were multiple, but drugs and music were recurrent themes.

Drugs

No one, as stated above, is born an armed robber; one must construct oneself so as to embody that identity. The men described many techniques and strategies to assist their transition into an archetypal 'armed robber' and the use of drugs—to manufacture confidence, to calm nerves, and to enhance euphoria—was common.

Jesse (22) explained that he would smoke 'ice'[3] before a robbery to 'build confidence' and make him feel 'invincible', whereas Maru (30) and his associates had devised the perfect 'robbery cocktail', comprising 'a bit of heroin to calm the nerves' and then, 'just before going in, we pass around a bit of coke to make you alert, you know, pick you up'. The vast majority of men had similar approaches to drugs, favouring stimulants to augment the adrenaline. Tommy was an exception to this. He had been diagnosed with schizophrenia and would smoke cannabis before an armed robbery, concerned that anything else, particularly ice, would make him too volatile and violent:

> I used to like having a smoke of pot before going to do it. If I get on the ice and go and do a robbery, it becomes too violent. And I think about that, like, because I know, if I'm on the ice and my mental health's not right, you know, people are getting hurt, you know, and like, I didn't care . . . I look at it now, the drugs was actually what was giving me the confidence which is dangerous. I look at it now—it's the devil's drug; it's—it's the devil, you know, because what drugs do to people and what it's done to me and made me act, when I wouldn't usually act like that . . . So I try and just have a smoke of pot to keep it calm; just go in: 'Let's do this and let's go'. But, on the ice and me mental health, it's not a good mix, you know.

It was notable that the more professional armed robbers reported that they would never take drugs or drink alcohol prior to a hold-up as it could cloud their judgement. Greg (49), for example, stated that 'at no time would I go intoxicated; I wouldn't be under any influence'. Similarly, CK would never take any substances before an armed robbery, and said that after trying 'every drug every way' he was now mostly teetotal.

> I've had a few big nights on the alcohol, but I don't drink and I'm—I—you know, I've tried every drug every way. I might have a night on the coke

[3] Ice is a common street name given to crystal methamphetamine. It is a stimulant drug regarded as being stronger, cheaper, and more addictive than the powder form of methamphetamine known as speed. People describe the euphoric sensation from smoking ice as 'amping', as if they become an over-amplified wire.

after or smoked a bit of pot after a robbery. Heroin, once; I just vomited all night. I've shot up and I've done the lot, but it's just not for me. No, not for me. I'd rather go water-skiing.

Music: orchestrating criminal performance

'How's that song go?' Tommy had asked during the interview. 'Y'know, the one about "dollar bill y'all"?' The transcripts captured one of the more surreal moments in this study: '[*interviewer and interviewee begin to sing*]'—although, for accuracy, it really should have read: 'begin to sing, *badly*'.

Tommy listened to Wu-Tang Clan when preparing for a robbery because he claimed it got him in the right frame of mind. His song of choice was 'C.R.E.A.M.', with the apropos sentiment, 'Cash rules everything around me. C.R.E.A.M. Get the money. Dollar, dollar bill y'all'.

Just like the consumption of drugs, music has the capacity to elicit powerful emotions. Barthet and colleagues (2013: 228) highlight that music is often chosen 'for its ability to induce or convey emotions, which may manifest in anything from a slight variation in mood, to changes in our physical condition and actions'. As it does for many people, music has provided a soundtrack to my life—songs to cheer you up; songs to calm you down; music to soothe bereavements, to feed elation, to inspire, to channel anger; and those pieces of music that unexpectedly conjure up memories, whether good or bad. Music possesses an emotive charge, and so it is unsurprising that it also plays a pivotal role in the preparatory routines of armed robbers.

Like Tommy, Max (23) listened to rap and hip-hop music which, along with smoking ice, would assist him in embodying an armed robber and distract him from thinking too much about what lay ahead and all its potentialities.

It calms me down really. It stops me thinking like, 'What if the police come?' 'What if he bes a "hero"?' You know? 'What if, like, I have to shoot someone?' You know? I'm listening to that stuff, trying to keep that out of my head, yeah. I always have my phone tucked in my waistband and my earphones in listening to the music in one ear and the police scanner in the other.

There is a cyclical and iterative moral panic about music, dating back to the original conception by Stanley Cohen (1972) in relation to the mods and rockers of the 1960s, and perpetuated through, among other genres, punk, shock rock, gangsta rap, grime, and the latest headline grabber, drill (Savage, 2018). Much in particular has been made of the glamorization of gun violence, fast money, and disrespect for the law, especially in the rap and hip-hop music favoured by Tommy and Max. Rather less so the generative affect of Bosnian death metal. Maru and his associates had refined a very specific modus operandi; once pumped up with their cocktail of heroin and cocaine, they would don their blue overalls, paint the skin around their eyes black, and pull balaclavas over their heads. En route to the target, Maru told me, they only ever listened to Bosnian death metal, because it 'geed 'em up'.

So crucial did the music become in their preparations for armed robbery, Maru explained, that they had to make multiple copies of the soundtrack to their crime in different formats.

MARU: So, one of the guys was Bosnian and he used to listen to the music all the time and one day he brought it to boxing training and he played it and we just—all of a sudden, everyone loved it. We thought it geed 'em up, so, yeah. And because, um we used to send out these car thieves to go get the car for us, steal a car for us, yeah, some cars have, like, um, tape players; some cars had CD players. So, we made a disk and a tape for it, you know?

ET: You actually put together a mix of what you'd listen to on CD and a tape?

MARU: Yeah. It was in the newspapers, um, because we would leave the tape in [the car] or the disk in [the car] and the coppers, um they found it and—and it was like an ongoing thing that—for them—they thought it was evidence that they found the same music—same CD, same tape, same music on it.

The music, while effective in arousing the mood of the robbery gang, would eventually lead to their conviction for multiple offences, as they invariably forgot to retrieve their music from the getaway car before abandoning it. The police dubbed the gang the 'Yugo Bandits' (Bosnia having been part of the former state of Yugoslavia), and eventually used this evidence to connect several of their crimes together and successfully prosecute them.

It has been argued that 'extreme music', characterized by chaotic, loud, heavy, and powerful sounds, can produce expressions of anger and activate aggressive behaviours (Gowensmith and Bloom, 1997; Selfhout et al., 2008). Affect can be used to explore and understand the way in which props and artefacts are commonly used to aid the transformation into an 'armed robber'—fast cars, guns, intravenous needles, balaclavas, music—influence the scene and enable the transformation of those actors within it.

The sound of violence: vocabularies of robbery

Kilby and Ray (2014: 4) note that violence is often depicted in scholarly texts as 'an impassioned yet silent phenomenon'; they believe that 'what perpetrators say before and during the act of violence requires closer attention'. Far from mute, the chosen words and the style of their delivery are important and revealing aspects of robbery.

Sammy reported that he would practise his phrasing and tone in the mirror in a bid to achieve as good a level of intimidation and command that a 12-year-old could muster (see 'Learning the ropes'). And as Jesse outlined above, much of the performance of robbery is about how the offender presents himself. For him, a large part of this was affecting a commanding voice, a lesson that Robert (51) learnt the hard way:

> I have run into a bank once and said it was a hold-up and no one paid any attention to me. Like, I look back now and laugh about it. I had to clear me throat and then scream it out again. Do you know what I mean? Like—I don't know what happened but, I ran in there, right, and said, 'Right, it's a hold-up'—blah, blah, blah, blah, blah—and everyone just kept doing what they were doing. Like, 'What the fuck?' Do you know what I mean? It was a bit—it was a bit surreal. Like really, 'What the fuck?' And I had to kind of, like, [*sound of clearing of throat*] clear the throat like that and then scream it out and—you know what I mean? I think it was more—not the—I think it was more the tone rather than the loudness that kind of got people's attention. Do you know what I mean? Maybe, like, the tone didn't imply a threat the first time, yeah. Maybe I was just too casual about it too. Do you know what I mean?

CK also outlined how verbal commands could direct the situation and create an atmosphere in which he had control:

> Bang! Gotcha, gotcha—whoa whoa—and then point the gun down straight away, because weapons are dangerous, you know; you want it

> pointed at the ground. And then, you know, calm it down—easy now—as soon as you get control. Drop your voice—whoa.

I couldn't help but note the similarities in CK's directives to the equestrian commands familiar from his days as a competitive show jumper and a professional polo player. His use of 'whoa' (a command often used to stop or slow a horse) and 'easy now' were particularly resonant of horse riding. The analogy between his sporting life and committing armed robbery was hard to ignore throughout my conversations with him; the skill he described drawing on to overcome obstacles, the showmanship, the speed and precision, the careful planning, even the promise of respect and substantial winnings—the two were synonymous in many ways.

Techniques of neutralization

Gresham Sykes and David Matza's (1957) article, 'Techniques of neutralization', argued that offenders use rationalizations to enable themselves to engage in criminal behaviour. Their propositions are themselves built upon Edwin Sutherland's (1947: 6–7) theory of Differential Association, which contends that individuals engage in deviant behaviour when they are exposed to and internalize 'an excess of definitions favorable to violation of law over definitions unfavorable to violation of law'. Inscribed in these 'definitions' are rationalizations for deviancy, which play an important role in the genesis of criminal behaviour. Individuals draw upon neutralization techniques to protect their self-concept while committing delinquent acts, enabling them to 'drift' (Matza, 1964) in and out of delinquency and still maintain a general commitment to the prevailing societal values of 'right' and 'wrong'.

Sykes and Matza (1957) proposed five techniques of neutralization: denial of responsibility, denial of injury, denial of the victim, condemnation of the condemners, and appeal to higher loyalties.[4] Several scholars (Cornish and Clarke 1986; Cromwell et al., 1991; Taylor, 2014) have suggested that offenders often impose reconstructed or 'fictional rationality' (Matthews

[4] A further seven techniques have since been added: defence of necessity (Klockars, 1974), metaphor of the ledger (Minor, 1981), denial of the necessity of the law, the claim that everybody else is doing it, the claim of entitlement (Coleman, 1994), 'justification by comparison', and 'postponement' (Cromwell and Thurman, 2003).

2002: 38) on post hoc explanations of their offences, often utilizing techniques of neutralization to justify their actions when, in reality, their actions are more viscerally compelled, impulsive, and chaotic. In some cases, these justifications can become tangled with the etiology of criminal behaviour and play an important role in maintaining persistence in crime (Hirschi, 1969; Maruna and Copes, 2005; Taylor, 2014). In other words, excuses and justifications developed and refined over time serve to shape the offender's particular offence chain and a post-offence rationalization in one instance may become an enabling neutralization technique in another. As Stanley Cohen explains in *States of Denial* (2001: 61), offenders use their chosen justification narrative to mentally 'prepare the ground for the offence to take place'.

'We're very good at justifying bad behaviour,' Robert tells me with a smile, as he leans back in his chair. He admitted that although he'd pretend he was committing crime to support his mum, this was actually a way of alleviating his guilt.

> You start off first and you pay the bills for your mum—you know, the old bills on the fridge. Then you try to give your mum money. But that doesn't last too long, because they actually start getting honest with themselves and realizing where the money's coming from. It's handy for 'em, so they might accept it at first, not wanting to believe where it comes from. But, once they are honest with themselves, then they don't want the money, because it's dirty money. So they don't want to encourage you, because it's very easy to justify to yourself by saying, 'I'm helping the family'. Do you know what I mean? Like, we're very good at justifying bad behaviour, yes. Do you know what I mean?

Some would construct elaborate excuses and justifications for their crimes, developing a personal code of ethics. Sykes and Matza (1957: 665) outlined how offenders 'often draw a sharp line between those who can be victimized and those who cannot' and frequently hold that certain social groups are not considered 'fair game'. In this study, there were several of these neutralizations that centred on gender, in particular deliberately not targeting females, if it could be helped. For example, Josh (29) avoided commercial robberies when women were working, explaining, 'I grew up with a single mum and I never targeted shops that had women or young girls at the counter, you know'. Cameron (27) held similar chivalrous views:

> I wouldn't do it if there was a female there. I don't know, how can I put it—I just wouldn't put a female through that, because it can be quite scary—someone coming at you like that. I just think a man might handle the situation a bit better, yeah. I just wouldn't like doing it to a female, I guess, that's all.

Denial of injury was a common theme among the robbers, who would often refer to the businesses having insurance. Jez (49) would remind his victims of this in a bid to convince them to hand over the money, telling them: 'This is an armed robbery. Just comply and no one's going to get hurt. Your money's insured so don't be silly.' David (34) similarly utilized well-versed neutralization techniques by initially 'denying the victim' because they would be compensated through insurance, before 'appealing to a higher loyalty' by suggesting that the business practices of clubs were immoral and therefore eclipsed his own wrongdoing:

> I don't think it's—it's wrong to steal off, um, businesses that are insured, businesses that are making a killing from other people's, um, mishaps—like gamblers, alcoholics—like, pubs and clubs. I don't know; I don't know if that makes any sense.

CK was a little more reticent to explain away his behaviour as being guided by a moral compass. He did comment, though, that when he had targeted the clubs and noticed that a lot of the haul comprised pensioners' cheques, like David above, this relieved his guilt a little; the clubs didn't hold any moral high ground.

CK: Well, I'd see the big clubs with their poker machines. I thought, 'Oh'—you know—'you're robbing everybody.' I—I—I've no sympathy for banks, although I have sympathy now for the people whose space I invaded because I—I can see that it's—it's real—it would be pretty frightening, you know.

ET: So did you feel that there was a certain moral aspect to the places that you would target, like big businesses?

CK: Oh, look, I'm not going to go quite that far. But I used to think, you know, when I'd be burning all the pensioners' cheques and that—because I'd get—you'd get all that and you'd see that they'd cashed their cheques at the club—I'd think to myself, 'I wonder if he gave 'em any money to go home with,' you know, as they'd put it all in the poker machines. So I'd have—you know, that's about as principled as I got. Armed robbers aren't usually that principled; you know, it's more based on greed.

ET: So did you feel justified in any way hitting the pokies?

CK: Nah, nah, nah; nah, nah, nah; nah, nah. I—I don't think you can be justified. Even if I—I—I robbed a—a drug dealer, I don't think you can be justified.

These justifications fit neatly into the 'condemnation of the condemners' neutralization technique, whereby the robbers divert attention to the victims who are cast as hypocritical and devious; 'by attacking others, the wrongfulness of his own behavior is more easily repressed or lost to view' (Sykes and Matza, 1957: 668).

Scott (34) thought that robbery was more 'honourable' and less 'sneaky' than other crimes such as breaking and entering and sex offences, and in doing so made 'justifications by comparison':

> People that do break and enter? They're—oh, I think they're like, um—um, weaker, I—I think—I don't know how to explain it—like, weaker. Like, they don't want people to be there. They don't want a confrontation and all that, you know. I think—they want to be sneaky, you know. I don't know. My armed robberies are a pretty respectable thing, I guess, in jail; yeah, it's pretty respectable. It's better than a lot of the other people in here, like sex offenders and whatever else you've got in here, you know.

The majority of offenders in this study mobilized neutralization techniques to some degree in order to attempt to make their offences understandable if not condonable. Over time, they are able to construct a self-schema that is moralistic and conscientious. Through the development of complex moral codes, burglars are able to navigate cognitive dissonance and dampen conflict between their self-concept as a moral person and their morally reprehensible behaviours.

Conclusion

Some studies have found that fathers disapprove of their son's offending (for example, Rowe and Farrington, 1997), yet the present study included several participants who were exposed to and involved in the criminal activities of their male relatives from a very early age. Some, indeed, such as Sammy, were actively recruited and trained to commit robberies. Even though the method of robbery was perceived in the most part to be very simple, there was a degree of preparation involved. Invariably this involved planning by the professionals, and getting into character for the amateurs, who tended to rely on props such as clothing and weapons to communicate that a robbery was taking place. Whereas most offenders seek not to be seen committing criminal acts, the modus operandi of the armed robber is one where they take centre stage, and this calls forth a certain degree of performativity.

For Billy, the dejected inmate in this chapter, armed robbery was self-actualizing and penetrated the fog that had descended over his life; the crime had become one of the few stimuli that actually 'made him *feel*'. Clearly, for some, the sensations experienced before, during, and after a robbery, and the status and respect it brings to one's identity, enabling them to transcend feelings of being a 'nobody', are delectable and compelling. In this way, crime can provide offenders with an opportunity to construct and inhabit a particular identity that would otherwise be unattainable. Many of the robbers had constructed self-styled moral codes in order to justify their offences and drew upon moral relativism to juxtapose their offence with those of others in an attempt to make it appear less serious. It is clear that the imposition of these self-regulated moral codes was a mechanism by which to justify and downplay their actions. Participants were eager to distance themselves from other types of offenders who they believed didn't possess the same criminal capital as them.

6
Doing Rob (and Getting Away with It)
Planning and Process

> It's not rocket science, armed robbery, you know. The thing about armed robberies—look, the beauty of an armed robbery is you're in and out where, like—say, if you break into, like, say, a factory, you're up in the roof; it's a lot of work and you have a long time in which you could be discovered. The armed robberies, you're in and out; right? But, in saying that, armed robberies can go wrong [*snaps fingers*] that quick. Do you know what I mean? They can go terribly wrong so quickly, you know.
>
> **(Robert, 51)**

> You just run in; say, 'Everybody get on the fucking ground. Everyone drops on the ground and then you grab—you grab one of the people from behind the counter; you put the blade up to their throat and you say, 'Look, open the fucking safe'. They—they open the safe for you. You bag up all the money and you leave; you're out of there.
>
> **(Billy, 20)**

Robbery might be straightforward, but it is never simple. In outlining the approaches to robbery, stark differences between those who might be considered 'amateurs' and those who might be considered 'professionals' come to the fore. Whereas the professional might spend weeks, if not months, meticulously planning a job, the amateurs, particularly the most drug- or alcohol-affected, would commit instantaneous impulsive robberies that were high risk and low value. Broadly speaking, there is a spectrum

Armed Robbers. Emmeline Taylor, Oxford University Press. © Emmeline Taylor 2022.
DOI: 10.1093/oso/9780198855132.003.0006

of methods ranging from very little preparation and a belief that anyone can 'do rob' given its crudity, through to the most professional and diligent planners who take pride in the mastery, competence, and contacts required for a lucrative heist.

The division is also reflected in the target choice, with the relatively organized robber identifying more profitable premises such as banks (although increasingly rarely), cash in transit, and betting shops, whereas the amateurs take a more opportunistic approach, holding up convenience stores, service stations, and fast food outlets. Further interrelated with organized/amateur distinctions and the target is the weapon selected; although knives are most commonly used in commercial armed robbery in Australia, the robbers reported a range of different weapons, including firearms, machetes, syringes, and baseball bats. Ranging from the chilling to the farcical, the final section of this chapter explores what happens when things don't go according to plan.

Banks to bottlos: changes in target selection

There are certain characteristics that robbers find appealing in a potential target. In interviews with commercial robbers, Swanson (1986) identified the five most desirable features: remote area, no customers, lone worker, easy access/getaway, and the promise of substantial money. Over the past few decades there has been a significant shift in the type of commercial premises that are typically targeted by armed robbers. For example, banks and financial institutions, once accounting for a large proportion of armed robberies, are now very rarely held up. In fact, they now account for less than 2 per cent of all robberies each year (Borzycki and Fuller, 2014). This shift in target—largely due to the sophistication of security technologies now routinely deployed in high-end commercial premises—throws into sharp relief the amateur robbers who go so far as to invert the rational calculus of the more organized 'professionals', in that they typically commit high-risk/low-value offences. Furthermore, the trend is not specific to Australia; similar changes have been reported in the USA, where the Federal Bureau of Investigation (FBI) figures for 2012 put the number of bank robberies nationwide at 3,870; the lowest in decades (Lee, 2013). Likewise, the British Bankers Association (BBA) reported a 90 per cent reduction in armed robberies between 1992 and 2011.

There were some old-school bank robbers in the sample, particularly, Jez, Robert, and CK, who, not coincidentally, were also the oldest people that I interviewed; 49, 51, and 62 years old respectively. They were committing their high-end robberies more than a decade ago, and despite their experience and accumulated knowledge gained through extensive criminal careers, they recognized that banks have become more difficult to rob and a lot less lucrative. Robert acknowledged that banks used to be a lot simpler and didn't involve much planning, so long as the perpetrator had firearms:

> It was a lot easier back in those days; you could actually drive up to the street, there's the bank (*indicates*), put your balaclavas on and run in and run out. I'd only be pissing in your pocket if I said, you know, a lot of planning went into it. It was more like, you know, we got the gun and we got car and we go: 'Let's do it.' Do you know what I mean?

As ever, just as one criminal behaviour falls out of favour, another approach quickly emerges to replace it. While the victimization rate of banks and financial institutions has dramatically decreased, there has been a corresponding increase in the targeting of 'softer' commercial targets such as liquor stores (known colloquially in Australia as 'bottlos'), service stations ('servos'), hotels, pubs, clubs, supermarkets, fast food outlets, and restaurants (Mouzos and Borzycki, 2003). Illustrating this tactical displacement, between 1993 and 2000, the incidence of armed robbery of service stations in Australia increased by 214 per cent (Australian Institute of Criminology, 2002). The perceived ease with which service stations and convenience stores can be held up have earned them the nickname 'stop and robs' among some offenders (Petrosino and Brensibler, 2003). As a result of this effortlessness, some participants, such as Jayden (25), scornfully attested that robbing service stations was just a 'junky's crime'. It is important to recognize that although armed robbery overall has been in decline across Australia, this obscures the fact that some types of target are actually undergoing an increase in victimization as offenders refocus their energies.

How the change in target selection has instigated a parallel change in the conduct and performance of offences remains poorly understood. In reference to trends in Britain, Wright et al. (2006: 1) point to 'increasing evidence that the situational dynamics of robberies in Britain are changing, with offences becoming correspondingly more spontaneous and desperate'. Not only has the situational profile of armed robbery shifted dramatically, so has the profile of offenders. Hobbs (1995: 9) observes that armed robbery, once regarded as having a measure of professional conduct, has descended 'into haphazard, essentially amateur excursions featuring minimal planning, a low level of competence, and a lack of commitment'. Similarly, Matthews (2002: 22) attests:

> Contrary to popular opinion, the largest group of known commercial robbers are not the sophisticated career robbers who meticulously plan and execute their crimes but a motley group of amateurs and novices who engage in little planning and often seem unaware of the consequences of their actions. These amateurs are generally characterised by their low level of organisation, their selection of more accessible targets, their lack of experience, their relation to violence and their use of weapons. They will tend to operate alone, they aim for relatively small amounts of money and they have had a history of 'failed' or 'attempted' robberies. In many cases the robberies appear as little more than acts of desperation, usually because the person needs money quickly to pay off debts, to buy necessities or to support a drug habit.

Disentangling these offenders from the broad taxonomy of 'armed robbery' raises some pertinent questions about target selection, modus operandi, and anticipated rewards. David (34) stated 'if I was born 20 years earlier, through the seventies and eighties, I'd definitely be doing banks. But now? It's just stupid'. Similarly, Jesse (22) declared that he would 'never be able to get away with' robbing a bank, because

> they've set up a lot of plans, you know, and they've got the fly-up thing and it's just too high a risk. If you get caught for doing a bank, you'll get a lot more [longer sentence] than you would for doing a pizza shop.

Ben (19) had developed a penchant for fast food outlets, because 'they make heaps of money' and yet they do not have anywhere near the same level of security as banks:

> Ah, KFC, Red Rooster; just all the main ones, like, take-away stores . . . Like, people go there all day, every day, and give 'em, like, notes and stuff and, at the end of the week, you can get lots of money off 'em. McDonald's, like all the famous places—you know.

Similarly, Billy committed 'spur of the moment' robberies and was not amenable to the planning that a bank robbery would entail. Instead he was more interested in '[t]he TABs[1] and the clubs . . . If I want quick cash, probably, like, fast food restaurants, like Kingsley's or KFC or McDonald's or something like that.' But sometimes desperation, particularly for drugs, would override any sensible and rational decision making. For example, Billy explains that some locations were very high risk:

> Say, if it was in, like, the middle of the city, you know, I wouldn't do it because of how—how much things are around me—do you know what I mean? Because there's clubs, there's hotels, there's the cop shop, there's the courthouse, there's—just lots of things like that, you know, that'd turn me off doing it. But then, if I was feeling bad enough, I'd still do it; do you know what I mean? So—so, if I needed the drugs there and then, I'd go do—I'd go do it, wherever it was.

Given the spontaneity of the robberies committed by the more amateur and drug-affected robber, it was not surprising that correspondingly very little planning had gone into maximizing the chance of success and the likelihood of significant financial reward. The offenders were mixed in their approach to reconnaissance and planning, with some spending several months researching the target, while others hadn't given it a thought until they were on the premises demanding cash.

Planning

Despite its significance for understanding the mindset of the criminal subsequent to committing an offence, few studies have examined the extent to which violent crimes are planned. Furthermore, those that have done so have produced widely disparate estimates of planning, mostly because they rely on different measures of what constitutes organization and preparation (see Birkbeck and LaFree, 1993; Gill 2000). For example, Petersilia et al. (1978) found that 25 per cent of robbers reported that they had planned

[1] TAB stands for the Totalisator Agency Board, and was the name given to racing and sports-betting agencies in Australia and New Zealand. Originally government owned, most have been privatized. The term denotes a club that has an on-site betting agency, and usually a bar, restaurant, and poker machines.

their offence in detail, 50 per cent planned some aspect of their crime, and 25 per cent did not plan at all. Walsh (1986) found that just over half of armed robbers planned their offence, while Feeney (1986) found that only 15 per cent engaged in some degree of planning. However, while many robbers appear to commit their crime on impulse and as opportunities present themselves, they are much more likely than other types of violent offender to explicitly plan their offences for obvious reasons (Felson and Massoglia, 2012). There is also the possibility that offenders impose, consciously or not, a reconstructed 'fictional rationality' (Matthews, 2002: 38) on post hoc explanations of their offences when in reality they were more viscerally compelled, impulsive, and hectic.

Tommy (24) insists that due to the number of variables and the unpredictability of how people will act, it is impossible to plan for a robbery:

> You can't plan for a robbery; you know what I mean? You just don't know; you can only assume what's going to happen. You don't know what's going to happen when you walk in the door. It doesn't matter how much planning you put into it; you don't know what you're going to face. It's very unpredictable.

Yet, for the professional armed robber, it is precisely the eradication of this unpredictability that is their core business. In a well-planned robbery everything has already been foreseen, each factor and actor identified, and their role mapped out in detail so that when the time comes the robbery unfolds as if it were a scripted play.

CK described the importance of planning so as to remain calm during the robbery and not have to think on your feet: 'when you plan something and plan it properly, once you step over the point of no return, it's like automatic'. He outlines below the process of planning the robbery of an Australian club.[2]

[2] A 'club' in this context would be a venue with multiple activities on offer—live sports televised on large overhead screens, extensive gambling stations with pokies, a bar, and restaurant—such as an RSL club. The Returned and Services League, Australia (RSL) set up clubs initially for current and former Defence Force members to provide services for members, including fostering an environment for the protection and promotion of the ideals of the Anzac spirit and heritage (traditionally, at 6 p.m. each evening, 'The Ode of Remembrance' was read, followed by one minute's silence to honour those who died serving their country). Over time, these commercial entities, known generally as RSL Clubs (but also called Ex-Services, Memorial, Legion, or other similar names), generated huge profits. Today the service clubs are a multi-billion-dollar industry employing thousands, with a 40 per cent share of NSW's $3.2 billion of annual gaming machine profits. See Brown (2014) for interesting insights on the changing role of RSL clubs in Australia.

> If you're doing clubs, then it's going to be at closing. So it'll be a Sunday night at closing, when the maximum amount of money's there. So you—you—you would look then for the Director because the Director's going to have the keys to the vault. He's going to be the bloke that's in charge of the safe and he's usually got his name written in the car park. So you'll see that that's the chap. Now, you've already watched him a few times and you've seen how the place closes and how it locks down and who goes where and what goes what because, if everything's not the same, I don't move. Over a month, that's how I build my confidence. I look. I sit. And then I'd go up the street and sit with binoculars. 'Yeah, she works in the chemist; yeah, that's the bloke from the fish and chip shop; yeah, that's the guy; yeah, there's the manager'. So on the day I would, at maybe three in the morning, put the car that's going to be used in the robbery in place with all the gear in it. Then [I'd know] so-and-so should be coming now; so-and-so should be coming now, and I'd be saying to whoever's here, 'Right, it's nearly time'. As soon as he [the manager] comes, 'you go down and drop me here' and then I'd go to the car, pick up whatever I want out of the car and stroll in.

There were many similarities between CK and Jez's description of how he went about planning his robberies of banks and post offices, particularly regarding the surveillance of targets preceding the robbery:

> It's just common sense really. You know, you just had to plan ahead. So, um, you want somewhere where ah, when the emergency button is pushed in the bank you know the radius to the nearest police station. You're looking on a map and you're looking at also having two-way radios as well and scanners so you know where the patrol car is. So you can pick up where the patrol cars are and at what time. Um, also, um, what you do is you—you pick a time when they're [police] doing changeover shifts as well, so that takes up time because they're actually back at the station. You got to do your homework; it's the same time every day.

The type of homework that the robbers would do varied, but it was about having as much prior knowledge about the target as possible. 'The internet is a wonderful thing,' Liam (31) told me with a wink. He would not commit a robbery unless he had 'inside intel', and although he wouldn't tell me how he recruited his sources, he divulged that it was usually a friend who knew someone who knew someone. A key piece of information he would extract from the insider was the location and make of the safe:

> I want the safe. I've got the tools, I just need the design and make. I research it on the internet—it will tell you everything. Everything. Down to how much it weighs, its circumference. You could even go and buy an exact replica of the same safe, you know, have one delivered to your door.

The more professional robbers in the sample shared significant disdain towards the impulsive amateurs. CK was not impressed with the inexpert and sloppy armed robbers who did little, if any, planning and reconnaissance:

CK: They're not capable of robbing banks. Banks are the same to rob today as they were when I was doing 'em. Just as easy. Just as easy; for me, it is.
ET: Why do you think these guys are not capable?
CK: Well, they haven't even got a gun. They can't—they're not connected. They can't get access to any of the equipment required. They wouldn't know how to use a scanner; they wouldn't know where to get the frequencies, even if they did get one. You know, they don't know what night vision binoculars are; they don't know what surveillance is. It takes me a month to do a robbery. They want to do one—they—they—they walk—they think 'I'm going to do a robbery' and five minutes later they're doing one.

Like CK, Chris drew a distinction between the professional skilled experts who planned their crime and the reckless offenders who committed spur-of-the-moment hold-ups for very little financial gain. He had been convicted of conspiracy for the detailed planning of a robbery and was serving up to 6.5 years. Prior to his conviction he had been employed as a Loss Prevention Officer for a large retailer and had utilized the inside knowledge he had gained to assist with the planning of a robbery, conducting what he referred to as a 'risk assessment':

> Basically, if you're doing risk assessment, you pick the location, the police station, the estimated response time from a panic button or a phone call and for them to get to you and you to get to somewhere where you can get away. So there's a lot of planning that goes into it in order to make sure [of] your success . . . So, when I do a risk assessment, you have

> to weigh up the chance of getting caught, the money you're going to get from it and whether it's worth doing; so there are those three things. So, if you look at it—in the conspiracy that I got done for, I did a risk assessment, so I could get out of doing the actual crime; I thought, 'Oh, well, I'll do this and then you guys can go for it.' I got sentenced for the planning of it.

The day of the interview was Chris's 36th birthday and he'd been ruminating about his sentence, feeling particularly resentful that he hadn't physically committed the robbery, yet he was still given a lengthy custodial sentence. He was aggrieved, more specifically, that the planning he'd put into it resulted in his conviction, whereas, in contrast 'junkies' were wreaking havoc and giving everyone a bad name. Chris was annoyed about the way in which robbery in Australia had descended into what Hobbs, cited above, described as incompetent 'amateur excursions' and lamented that drug-affected offenders were undermining the skill of armed robbery:

> Look; most of the servos are done by little ice junkies that have no concept of time, so they think it up and they say, 'Let's do it' and it's done. And most of the time they aren't prepared, and they go with whatever they can get: a pocketknife or a pair of scissors or a syringe . . . All the runabouts, all the users: they'll do it just for a free hit; and that's where the idiots come from that give us a bad name.

Chris was not the only one with inside knowledge of retail security practices. Jayden (25) was serving 3.5 years for an aggravated robbery, estimating that he had committed 'four or five' robberies at shops and RSL clubs. He had worked as a security guard in several clubs and a shopping mall, and explained that he had 'learnt everything' through the training he received to assist with planning his robberies. In addition, he told me that he would regularly receive inside information and tip-offs from other security officers, including:

> When the money gets picked up and how much; when they open the safe; when's the best time to do it—like, when there'll be the least amount of people in the store; so what time is the best time; and the location of the safe and everything you need to know, so you can just run straight in there and do what you need to do and get out.

Clearly this level of insider knowledge is very valuable, greatly reducing the risks involved in committing a commercial robbery. According to Jayden, bar the 'odd one', all security guards are 'dodgy'. He attributed this to those in the profession earning minimum wage while working long and often unsociable hours in a job that could often be stressful and dangerous. This assertion is grounded in some truth; over 40 years' research on private security officers 'presents a consistently disappointing picture of working life' (Nalla and Wakefield, 2014: 735). It would appear that not a huge amount has changed since these findings, which suggest that low pay scales in concert with long working hours inhibit the recruitment of high-calibre and long-term employees, resulting in high staff turnover and therefore a lack of commitment or loyalty to the job.

At the other end of the spectrum from the planners, the more amateur, impulsive, and—typically—drug-affected robbers did not engage in any planning prior to the robbery, relying on surprise and intimidation. For example, Matt (27) described himself as 'an opportunist' who committed 'spur of the moment' robberies. He had become very casual about his offences, so much so that on one occasion he had robbed a service station because he had left his cigarettes at a friend's house. Passing a servo, he went in with a kitchen knife and left with 91 cartons of cigarettes. Robert (51) had 'lost count' of how many robberies he had committed (but had been convicted for five); he refuted the idea that he and his co-offender engaged in any rational thinking or forward planning: 'there were two heads but no brain between us. There was no reasoning or rational thought there; we got the gun and we got the car and we go.'

Irrespective of whether any planning went into the commercial armed robberies, a common factor was that the offence was intended to be very quick. Matt (27) estimated that a robbery would take '30 seconds; literally just in and out', going on to explain that taking longer would only reap low-level rewards: 'look, you could stand there for 20 minutes and pack your bag full of chips and pies if you really wanna. It depends on what you're after, you know?' Yet some of the more financially rewarding crimes took longer than the impulsive till grabs that were synonymous with the drug-affected offenders. Jayden had spent approximately two months planning to rob a 'Labour club' and he estimated that the actual crime took five to ten minutes. He attributed much of this time to 'crowd control' in particular tying up the employees to prevent them from accessing the duress alarm or calling for help. Jayden and his accomplice escaped with $120,000 from that particular robbery.

Those who engaged in meticulous planning were in the minority in this sample and typically much older. The shift to softer targets exposed the crude and slapdash approach of many contemporary armed robbers. The differences also influenced the type of weapon that robbers used in their offences.

Weapon choice

Jesse (22) was adamant that with the correct demeanour, a weapon was not required:

> it doesn't really matter about the weapon, because people sometimes are just scared and they just hand over the money—because they're very intimidating. You've got—some people have a very intimidating voice and that and some people just hand over their money—without even using a weapon.

Similarly, Chris claimed: 'You can certainly rob somebody without a weapon and say, "This is a robbery; give me all your money or you're dead". As long as you say it with conviction, then you'll have the desired effect.' Likewise, Liam (31) relied on the universal symbolic artefacts of robbery to communicate to employees what was taking place:

> If you're going to do a bank, you know, there's people that are defending it with guns, so you'd want to take a gun. Do you know what I mean? If I was to walk into a phone shop, I wouldn't be taking a gun; I'd probably take nothing. Usually, like, if you—if I was going in in a balaclava, that's generally enough in those sort of places—because they're trained to just hand over the cash; do you know what I mean? A lot of businesses are like that. Usually a balaclava is enough.

Liam was confident that the majority of employees working for large household-name companies would have been well enough trained to perform their expected ritualized role of complying with the demands of a robber, armed or not. Josh (29) had learnt that staff working in a store that was part of a retail chain were relatively compliant compared to independent stores: 'if you hit a shop and it's the owner's they're usually pretty reluctant to hand over the money'. Cameron (27) knew this from first-hand experience working as a cashier at a supermarket chain:

> I used to work at Coles myself as a checkout operator and I remember back then they used to say, like, 'if someone comes in to rob the joint, just don't be a hero; just hand it over,' yeah, 'just let 'em be on their way and don't try to stop 'em and don't try to be a hero.' That always stuck in my head.

Murray (32) was of a similar view. Having been confronted with a machete by the store owner when he tried to rob a convenience store, he reported that he went on to only target pharmacies, because he 'knew that the chemist would be more professional in giving the money up' and that they are 'not the kind of people that'd keep weapons behind the counter'.

It is estimated that approximately half of all robberies are committed with some type of weapon. In 2013, just over half of armed robberies in Australia involved a knife (52 per cent), followed by 'other weapons' (20 per cent), and firearms (18 per cent). Collectively, bats/bars/clubs, bottles/glasses, and syringes were used in 10 per cent of all armed robberies (Australian Institute of Criminology, 2016). However, this covers all armed robbery and so obscures some of the more nuanced trends. Knives are the most frequently used weapon in armed robberies in Australia, but for some targets, particularly financial institutions and licensed premises, firearms are equally or more likely to be used (Borzycki, 2006).[3] It is, however, difficult to gain a definitive picture of weapon use, particularly with regard to ascertaining specific details such as, say, the type of firearm. Sometimes weapons are implied, rather than explicitly brandished, and unless a firearm is discharged—which is thankfully rare (O'Donnell and Morrison, 1997; Wellford et al., 1997)—or later recovered, its categorization is based either on the description provided by victims or witnesses or on CCTV footage.

Firearms

Police data suggest that the type of firearm used, at least in banks, has changed over time (Borzycki, 2003; Matthews 2002). Pistols were used

[3] For example, of the 11,698 robberies recorded during 2013, just under half, 5,628, were committed with some form of weapon (Australian Institute of Criminology, 2016).

more often than long arms in Australian bank robberies in the early to mid-1980s, but the reverse held true for the late 1980s. Then, between 1998 and 2002 pistols were once more used in the majority of robberies involving firearms (Borzycki, 2003), tracking trends observed for other violent crimes, such as homicide (Mouzos and Rushforth, 2003).

The most dramatic change in weapon use over time is among offender gangs (three or more offenders). In the 1980s almost all gangs used weapons during bank robberies, with pistols and long arms equally likely to be used. However, between 1998 and 2000, most bank robberies committed by gangs involved no weapon—just sheer intimidation and brute force—only around 10 per cent and 6 per cent involving pistols and long arms, respectively (Borzycki, 2003). This potentially reflects two key processes: the emergence of less-organized and -connected criminal gangs on the one hand, and, on the other, a shortage of firearms following several gun reforms sparked by the 1996 massacre at Port Arthur, Tasmania.[4]

Robbers who were targeting the more high-end commercial premises such as banks favoured firearms. CK was the most experienced armed robber in the sample and was, as he boasted, 'well connected'. Testifying to the seriousness of the offences he had committed (or not committed), he had received one of the longest-ever sentences handed down for armed robbery in Australia. Given the targets that he set his sights on holding up, only semi-automatic firearms would provide the requisite threat in order to succeed.

> Well, it depends; it depends. If you can—if you can—if you can; it's all black [clothing] and AK47s, if you can. If you can't, it's, you know, some sort of a handgun, but there'd be an AK47 in a bag—or something, an M1 carbine or something—something so that you can just go, 'Bang, bang, bang'. It's all about—I—I—I wouldn't shoot you to get the money, but I'd frighten the shit out of you. I'm not shooting you for the money; I'm leaving before that happens; all right? However, it's a fighting retreat. If somebody comes and they want to put a scene on, I'm going to put half a clip into the air and I'll tell you: no one—*no one* comes at AK47s or M1

[4] One of the world's worst massacres perpetrated by a single gunman took place at Port Arthur, Tasmania in April 1996, where 35 people were killed and many more seriously injured. Twelve days after the massacre, several gun control measures were introduced under the 1996 National Firearms Agreement by the prime minister, John Howard. The agreement also instigated a national gun buyback initiative which resulted in more than 640,000 firearms being surrendered.

> carbines; a 746 still makes a big bang, you know. Even police: they just go [*holds hands up*]—and then, well, you're gone.

The immediacy with which a firearm communicates the seriousness of the situation made it a preferred weapon among several of the participants. The 'illusion of impending death' (Wright and Decker, 1997: 1) that guns conjure was found to motivate victims more expediently than other weaponry. Kimsan (39) used a 'roscoe' (handgun) and reported only having to display it in order to gain compliance:

> All you have to do is display your arm; and, once you display that, the majority of people are going to comply. Do you know what I mean? They're—they're not going to go, 'Ooh, ooh, ooh,' and try and be a hero or whatever. Do you know what I mean? And, like I said, I'm not a violent person, You can tell people's demeanour by the way they act and talk and how they're going to react to it; it's as simple as that. It's, like I said, common sense. Do you know what I mean? So if I—if I come in and point a gun at you, you know automatically what you're there for and, you know, the reason is I want the money et cetera, et cetera and 'boom'.

David (34) liked to use a 'shotty' (shotgun) because 'a sawn-off does a lot of the talking'. He explained that not only was it more intimidating than his .38 pistol, but, rather disturbingly, 'a sawn-off with side-by-side barrel, well, worst-case scenario, if you did have to shoot it, you don't have to be—you know, you don't have to be a professional; you just pull the double trigger and it's just going to spray everywhere'.

Robert (51) explained that, although it 'sounds terrible to say it, the gun garnered respect'. He was concerned about using any other weapon (including a pistol, similar to David above) through fear of 'have-a-go heroes' attempting to tackle him:

> Straight away, people are like: 'It's a gun.' With a knife, you get that bravado. It's why I never did clubs or pubs: because of the Dutch courage with the drink. That's why I like the shotgun too: because it's a threatening thing. See, with a pistol, I—I used to think to myself: 'Pistols'—sometimes I used to think, 'Maybe I'll have to fire it to let people know it's a real gun.'

In line with findings reported by O'Donnell and Morrison (1997), several participants reported a concern that people would think that a pistol was a replica, forcing them to discharge it to prove otherwise. Whether a firearm is actually discharged or not, it presents an extremely scary threat for victims and any other individuals who witness the incident.

While the cultural imagery of armed robbery is a man with a balaclava or stocking on his head holding up a bank with a gun, some participants explained that they would deliberately not use a firearm due to fear of attracting a greater penalty if they were caught. In this respect, sentencing guidelines do appear to act as a marginal deterrent in weapon choice. Tommy, like Jesse and Liam above, was confident that his frightening demeanour would be enough to intimidate victims into compliance, but took a knife with him in case he needed to escalate the threat.

> I've been involved with guns before. I've never—I've never actually used a firearm for a robbery though. Using a firearm carries a lengthier sentence and I know that, a lot of the places I rob, I could walk in with bare hands and threaten 'em with no weapon and walk away with the money. So I just thought to meself, 'Well, I'll bring a little knife and, if something ends up happening, well then I'll have to stab the bloke and get the money and go.' Like, that's the only option, you know.

Ben (19) took the same view, opting to take a samurai sword to rob fast food outlets such as MacDonald's. He explained:

> if you're robbing like a Maccas or something where lots of young people work, you just take a sword. You want to try and take the most less-scary thing you can because ... you don't really want to take a gun, because the coppers will look at it more serious and then they will come after you really hectic.

As Ben and Tommy indicate, as well as availability, the decision regarding weapon choice was rationally calculated to be the least offensive weapon that could still enable the robber to successfully complete the offence. It was about generating maximum fear in the shortest amount of time so as to make a swift escape.

Knives

Knives, of all shapes and sizes, are thought to be the most commonly used weapon in armed robberies in Australia, reported in just over half of incidents. The popularity of knives was due to a number of factors, including the relative ease of obtaining blades over firearms. As Chris (36) explained, 'I mean, knives obviously come up [more often] because guns are a bit harder to get at the moment'. Others chose knives because 'they're scary looking'. Billy (20) would 'always' brandish 'a knife, a gun, or a machete' during an armed robbery and confirmed that generating maximum fear was the key to a swift robbery and quick escape: 'Yeah; just something so, you know, you get it done quick, so you're not sitting around, fucking around, for ages; you get it done real quick'. For some, guns could actually be more cumbersome, being relatively heavy compared to knives:

> If there's security guards you're going to want a gun. Do you know what I mean? ... so—yeah. If there's going to be a weapon in there, a gun, you'd want another gun—I'd want to have a gun ... Handgun. You don't want anything too heavy or too bulky or something; yeah ... Usually I'd use a knife because that's like a small arm. Guns are heavier and, you know, people tuck 'em in their belt, but they always fall out, you know—yeah; a bit of a hassle.
>
> **(Liam, 31)**

> I only had a cooking knife, so I was going to take that, but I thought, oh—I had these novelty knives ... Like a hunting knife or one that you put up on the wall ... Yeah; I used that and it was very scary looking, I thought, so it worked very well.
>
> **(Jesse, 22)**

Most offenders reported having a weapon of choice. Kai (27), by contrast, was more pragmatic and would happily use any weapon he could find at the time: 'meat cleavers, machetes, hammers, kitchen knives, baseball bats, you know, bits of metal and all of that sort of stuff. I just grab anything really. Go to the kitchen drawer and it's all there, you know; just take your pick.'

Not all weapons have the desired impact. Jesse (22) had experimented with multiple weapons and for one robbery decided to use a 'dirty needle'; he half-filled a syringe with his blood, intending to inform his victim, a young man working behind the counter in a pizza shop, that it was HIV-infected.

But the staff member did not take the threat seriously, partly perhaps due to the difficulty of reaching over the counter to complete the threat of injecting him with the syringe:

> I've used knives before. But, with the pizza shop, I didn't have a knife or anything so I—like, I do inject drugs, so I used a fit—like, a needle—because I thought—you know, I thought it would be—I'm a bit of an amateur compared to some people when it comes to armed robberies, but I thought, you know—a fit would be scary looking. He said, 'Are you serious?' I said, 'Yeah'—you know, I swore—and I said, 'Just effing hurry up.' And he—yeah; he sort of didn't take me seriously. And then he sort of moved over to grab a bottle out of the fridge—because, at this pizza shop, there's, like, a fridge thing behind the counter; and I wasn't going to jump the counter, because there was heaps of people behind there working. And he went to grab a bottle—and I don't ever want to hurt someone; I would never hurt anyone over it, just in case I got caught. And, yeah; as he went to grab a bottle, I just thought, 'Oh, well, stuff it; I'm out of here'—you know—and took off.

Illustrating a connection between weapon choice and target type, data from the National Armed Robbery Monitoring Program show that, although only used in a minority of offences—an average of 4 per cent between 2004 and 2010—when syringes are used in robberies, it is most commonly when targeting pharmacies (Borzycki and Fuller, 2014), suggesting that these crimes are typically carried out by drug-affected offenders. Chris (31) acquiesces: 'All the armed robberies at chemists and stuff like that: that's all drug related. Either they have a debt, which is a lot of it; or they have a habit.'

Use of violence

It is interesting to note that Jesse claimed that he would never hurt anyone in case he got caught, rather than through any moral reasoning about harming another individual. The use of violence was discussed at length in the interviews.

The very definition of robbery involves the use or threat of violence in order to coerce the victim to hand over money and goods. The threat—or use—of violence is required to be of a sufficient level that the response of the victim is immediate; in other words, there is no room for ambiguity as to whether the perpetrator will physically hurt the victim if they do not comply with their instructions. The robbers in this study described different approaches to how they typically exercised violence and the extent to which they were willing to go in order to exert control and achieve their desired outcome. The majority claimed that they deliberately approached their offences so as not to cause physical injury to victims or bystanders, supporting findings in other studies (O'Donnell and Morrison, 1997).

Jez prided himself on his manners. He would say 'please' and 'thank you' and try to calm the victims down. This was to ensure that the offence ran as smoothly as possible, or so he claimed, but also, in all likelihood, served to alleviate his own guilt about subjecting people to such a terrifying ordeal.

> I've never threatened anyone's life. I always say, 'Please'—you know—'do as you're told, your money is insured, and no one's going to get hurt.' I ain't going to scream at the top of my voice and cause attention, like an idiot: 'Get on the floor!' and scare the hell out of people. I just don't, because I know there's a lot of elderly people there as well. So what I do is I'll grab the bank manager, so to speak, and tell 'em, 'Listen'—real quietly, you know—you know, 'just go to the safe quietly and that's it; no one's going to get hurt.' And they're like, you know—I know they're—they're scared, but I wouldn't have hurt anybody; put it that way ... If you put too much fear in 'em, you get panic. When you get panic, you get disorder, and you don't want that.

I went on to ask Jez what was required to be an armed robber. 'A set of big balls,' he replied without hesitation before, remembering his manners again, adding, 'sorry, excuse my French.' He continued:

> You just need to be so confident. You got to be motivated and you got to be switched on. You got to have your wits about you. You got to keep cool and calm at all times and you can't, ah, you know, fumble or falter.

Ben (19) outlined how important it was to ensure that victims were frightened in order to get them to comply:

> Like. You just go in and you scare 'em; you scare 'em, yeah? And straight away you let 'em know that you're not here to muck around, so you hit 'em or you swing a knife at 'em. Anyone that does the slightest little mistake or anything you didn't want them to do you just hit 'em. You make

'em think that, if you don't do as you're told, you're going to die or get hurt. And then you get 'em really scared and they want to do whatever they can to get you to go away, so they open up the money.

Like Ben, CK explained how he would enter a robbery at the highest-level threat from the outset to ensure that there was absolutely no room for doubt among the victim or anyone else in the vicinity about their intentions. But having taken command, he would, as Jez did, attempt to calm the nerves of those in the premises.

When we'd hit them, we'd hit them hard and not—not to be—be aggressive constantly, but that first shock would be pretty—pretty intense. You know, you'd be sort of—well, one guy said it was like being grabbed by terrorists, and it probably looked like it. You know, the guys there with AK47s and—and all in black and stuff like that ... You raise your voice. Let 'em know that you're in charge: 'I'm in charge now,' you know. Let 'em see who you are; let 'em see that it's not a joke, you know, and then 'bang'. As soon as you get their attention: 'Now everyone relax. I'm only here to collect; that's all I'm doing. I'm just getting wages. Everyone's going to be all right. Everyone relax. You, go around there.' Take control, start directing. Speak to the manager, call him by name if you know it; call him by name: 'You; I'm dealing with you, Mr So-and-so; you stay up. Everyone else around, flat on the floor, hands out.' You know, stay calm—if you're—if you're calm—you got to take the threat off 'em quick because they're frightened and they're going to do something out of fear. So, the quicker you get the threat off them, the quicker they're going to—they're going to stabilize; otherwise, they're edgy and they don't know what to do, so they think they'll—they think they'll run or—you know? So, as soon as you get the threat off 'em—the quicker you do that—the quicker they'll be able to gather their thoughts. You know, like, if I can get control with less—less is more. It's the same as riding show jumpers.[5]

[5] CK recurrently described the robberies he committed as similar to the process of show jumping—he had been a professional polo player and show jumper. It was interesting to hear the way that he drew these parallels, particularly in relation to the affective sensations he experienced. This is explored in further detail in Chapter 8.

The majority of participants insisted that although they attempted to radiate imminent threat and personify violent menace, they would never use violence or only resort to actual physical harm as a last resort.

Escalating duress on non-compliant victims

Although now dated, prior research has suggested that 30 per cent of victims do not comply with the demands of armed robbers (Luckenbill, 1981; Wellford et al., 1997). In such cases, an offender may seek to increase duress in order to force compliance with what he perceives to be a defiant victim. Robert (51) described the gear changes he would go through in order to escalate duress on non-compliant victims:

> Most times having a weapon would get the desired results. Sometimes, you might get someone who has a little bit of bravado and you have to, kind of like, assert your authority a bit—do you know what I mean? I did it gentlemanly. How should I say it? You've got to be—when I say 'nasty', you've got to be a bit forceful with 'em. Do you know what I mean? Like, you have to kind of go to that next step, where it's not like, 'Sit down, please.' Do you know what I mean? The next step might be, you know, 'Fucking sit down or I'm going to fucking shoot you'—right? Then, if they're still going on, it might be a—a bit of violence just to kind of—because you—you just—you take it to the next level to let people know, 'I'm prepared to'—'I'm going up levels.' Do you know what I mean? Until they get to the stage where they start thinking, 'Well, this—this isn't a joke any more.'

Robert told me that he had used his gun to hit his victims if he felt that they were not being compliant, but only as a near 'last resort'.

> That's usually kind of—I won't say 'last'; last resort's obviously shooting someone. But, you're getting very close to the last resort; do you know what I mean? That's kind of like things are getting very quickly out of hand. Say, like, you and me are doing something and—I'll give you an example. I might be over the counter, getting the money, but suddenly I've realized you've got no control of the room. So it has to—has to—things have to be kind of—I won't say 'balanced' but, yeah, before it gets out of hand—because, you know, like, people are very—they get—you know

> that mass hysteria thing. They either get mass hysteria or they get mass brave, yeah. That's why I'm thinking: I've found if you get one or two people who are a bit belligerent, the whole room will turn belligerent. That's—yeah; I'm not sure if that's the correct way of saying it, that's when you have to get a little bit—like, throw your weight around a little bit. That's the best way to say it, yeah. And, as I said, you always have the last resort.

Individuals who do not immediately do as instructed were the focus of much scorn and derision among armed robbers. Here Billy outlines how he 'had' to shoot an incredulous store manager in order to achieve compliance with his demands:

ET: Have you ever fired a gun when you've been in a robbery?
BILLY: Yeah; once, I *had* to.
ET: What happened?
BILLY: I shot him in the leg; yeah. He—he just told me—you know, he said, 'I'm not opening the safe', and then I said, 'Open it or I'll fucking shoot you,' and he goes, 'That's not a real gun.' So, I went 'bang' and shot him in the leg and then—yeah. Didn't get much out of that either.
ET: How did you feel afterwards?
BILLY: I felt so bad. Like, you know, that—that's probably crippled him for life. You know, shooting someone in the leg. That's bad; you can't be doing that.
ET: So would that put you off taking a gun now, do you think?
BILLY: Not really. I mean, I can't say I won't do it again, if you know what I mean? Like, if the same situation happened, I'd probably do the same thing again. But, you know, it's—it's something I don't want to do. But, if I *have* to, then it's the only way to get money; you know what I mean?

Similarly, Maru (30) describes *having* to hurt a bank manager in order to ensure that he would comply with the robbery gang's instructions not to alert the Armaguard security detail arriving:

> There was a TAB that we did, um, and Armaguard rocked up and that—so that put us on high alert because, like, oh, we had to hurt the—I had to keep the, um—the manager quiet. Um, we had to make him—because, um, they had a system where the manager had to, like, speak to the Armaguard and give 'em a password, say certain stuff to the Armaguard

for them to, you know, come in and take the money and whatever and, because they were armed, like, that was very heated that—that moment. And we had to time it because, if we—if there was any—like, if they had any suspicion, the cops would have been there in no time, you know. So we had to—we—the boys had—like, we had to hurt the, um—the manager to make sure he didn't—he said the right stuff . . . The boys broke his fingers; we broke his fingers with the gun. Oh, that was a do or die situation because, ah, it's either us or them, you know. There would have been a shoot-out if, you know . . .

Tommy's volatility and propensity to violence concerned him. Having been exposed to violence from an early age (see 'Criminal transmission' in Chapter 5), he was sometimes concerned that he might take things too far during a robbery.

TOMMY: I've been a very angry kid. The way I was brought up, I've been very violent; there's always been violence around me. I've seen a lot of domestic violence—normal, like, you know, violence and drugs and weapons and a lot of police activity in me life, so I've been very angry. So, when I'd lash out or become violent, it'd release a lot of that and—[I'd] just reach exploding point, you know, yeah.

ET: Did you find sometimes that you'd gone further than you thought you would?

TOMMY: Yeah, yeah, because it's unpredictable, as I said, with crimes like that. You know, like, you go in and a lot—a lot of the time I was polite; I'd say thank you to them when I'm leaving: like, 'Thank you, sir; I'm going,' you know, but—but, yeah. Like, I don't know if I'm going to walk into a place and not be arrested for a murder—you know, a robbery and a murder; like, you just don't know, you know, and these days, a lot of 'em fight back too, you know. And the way I used to look at it was: 'I'm not leaving without the money.' Like, that's the only option: 'You either give me the money or I'll attack you,' you know. . . . It's frustrating when you run in and you go, 'Put your hands up,' and they're, like—like, white as a ghost, it's—you know—'All right, look, just give me the money, it's'—you know—'fill the bag; I'm out of here.' But then you get other ones where you run in and they grab brooms, they grab bats and they try and fight you off and, you know—and then you just jump over the counter and just say, 'Look—look, man, don't'—you know—'stop stuffing around. You hit me with that'—right—'I'm going to have to put this'—you know—'this knife in your fucking head.' It's only when they start hesitating that I'd get violent, you know. I'd—I'd say, 'Look, you got 20 seconds, or I'm going to cut your fucking head off.' Do you know what I mean?

Tommy's concern about his behaviour and lack of control was not unfounded. He described becoming enveloped by rage when encountering recalcitrant victims and it was these moments that now appeared to him in recurrent flashbacks in his prison cell (see 'Shame and Guilt' in Chapter 8). Several of the men described trying to retain control of their anger as it teetered on a knife edge, allowing it to soar to a point of intense threat, but pulling it back before it tipped over into unconstrained ferocity. Similarly, Ellis et al. (2017) note in their study of violent male offenders that some would attempt to avoid situations that might prompt a loss of control since, once triggered, they were concerned about the severity of what might ensue.

In addition to victims failing to do as requested, not carrying out instructions fast enough was also reported to increase the likelihood of violence. Billy (20) described the anger he felt when he perceived the shopkeeper to be deliberately putting money in the bag slowly:

> It makes you raging. It makes you angry. It makes you feel like you want to shoot someone, you know, when they're taking forever. I just hit one over the back of the head and said, 'Hurry the fuck up'—you know—like, 'You're taking too long.'

As Matthews (2002: 38) notes, in relation to his study in England, 'the gratuitous use of excessive violence as a consequence of poor planning or limited co-operation on the part of cashiers or bystanders can hardly be seen as a strategy for maximising rewards and minimising punishments'.

At times, the reported reluctant use of violence—the mantra of 'nobody gets hurt'—was referred to as a kind of criminal code of conduct among armed robbers. While the majority probably genuinely didn't want anyone to get hurt during a robbery, this line appeared to be as much to do with self-preservation as it was a misplaced self-perception of compassion. Robert summarized the multiple factors that underscored not wanting to discharge the shotgun that he used in robberies or physically hurt anyone:

> Look, when you do an armed robbery, you don't want to fire a round off, because you know it's more time. Do you know what I mean? And, you know, the last thing you want to do is for the ricochet to hit someone.

> Do you know what I mean? So you—look, part of you doesn't want to hurt people because you don't want to hurt people; part of it is because you know you're suddenly looking at very big sentences and—do you know what I mean? Once you start running around with guns, shooting people and police are looking for you—they come looking for you with guns. We're going back to the stage here where, you know, it wasn't uncommon for police to try to shoot you and all that, yeah. If they saw you with a weapon, then, well, yeah. I mean, it was a bit of a different world then. I know it seems a bit fancy—fanciful, but it was a different world then—do you know what I mean—yeah. Like, yeah, they could almost—you know, like, not too many questions would be asked if they shot you, yes? Do you know what I mean?

Wannabe heroes

If there's one thing armed robbers do not like it is a 'wannabe hero': a member of the public or loyal employee who decides to tackle the criminal and try to prevent them from leaving the premises with their haul. As Liam (31) explained, 'the biggest threat when you're doing an armed robbery is someone trying to be a hero'. The visceral disdain with which the men in this study described these individuals revealed a collective contempt. They had all experienced one of these 'do-gooders' at some point in their criminal career. Josh (29) explains:

> Most people are pretty compliant, you know; they've got families to go home to, you know, like. But you get the odd one, I guess, or some hero coming in the store and, you know, he grabs a bottle off the counter or something and throws it at you. You know, like, you get—you always get some hero, but—yeah. I know most stores—yeah; they'll just—they'll give you the money, you know, rather than take the risk of getting hurt, you know, because they don't know how far that other person's prepared to go to get the money; whereas you do, you know. You might think, 'Oh, fuck; I'm glad she just gave me the money,' or, 'I'm glad he just gave me the money because I was going to turn around and walk out,' you know. But they don't know that, you know, so they're as scared as you are walking into the shop, I guess.

Of course, claiming that they would never actually use physical violence unless the victims or bystanders ('wannabe heroes') *made them* is just one of several mechanisms through which robbers can justify their actions to themselves and others. Holding their victims responsible is a well-documented trait of male domestic violence offenders; abusive men frequently blame their aggression on a range of external factors such as their partner's behaviour or substance abuse (Henning and Holdford, 2006). Similarly, the men in this study commonly attempted to minimize their culpability for physical violence by blaming their victims for not doing what they wanted them to.

While most tried to downplay the use of violence and fervently denied any suggestion that they might derive enjoyment from scaring or even harming their victims, a few did admit to gaining pleasure from witnessing the response that their violent acts elicited in others. As Will (41) described,

> There's no greater feeling than being 14 years of age and you're watching a grown man that's, like, on steroids and all that standing there, pissing himself, because you've got a gun pointed at him. Do you know what I mean? You just think, 'Oh, fuck, wow! I'm the one holding all this power now,' you know.

It's also important to point out that not all harm is physical. Many of the men were of the view that so long as there was no physical injury then the robbery was relatively victim-free. Some offenders were genuinely surprised that the fear they instilled in some victims could have very serious consequences, even in the absence of physical contact violence. Jack (37) reported being a little surprised that although he had been very polite during his robberies and only used what he described as 'low-level violence', the judge had sentenced him to 8.5 years, which during sentencing he had attributed in part to the 'emotional and psychological damage' that his offences inflicted on victims and witnesses. The mental health consequences of suffering violence and/or the threat of violence in the workplace has been linked to post-traumatic stress disorder, panic attacks, and anxiety (Taylor, 2019).

Security considerations

The few studies that have previously explored the process and planning of armed robberies now predate some significant changes in point of sale technology and security developments, not least closed-circuit television (CCTV), cash dye packs, security screens, and the growth in contactless payment reducing the circulation of cash. It is not known to what extent robbers consider these security hurdles and attempt to navigate them, but the offenders in this study described the techniques that they used. Below, CCTV, indelible dye packs, and the use of police radio scanners are explored.

CCTV

Few, if any, crime-control technologies have caused more controversy than CCTV. Millions of dollars have been spent, and much written, in attempts to establish whether it is effective in tackling crime. Some assert that it can act as a deterrent for would-be offenders. The crux of the deterrence capability lies in the claim that offenders are rational beings who weigh up the benefits and risks of committing a criminal act. Rational choice theorists assert that the rational criminal will execute the course of action that maximizes gain whilst minimizing risk and the potential for loss (Becker, 1968; Cornish and Clarke, 1986). If CCTV is known to be present, and interpreted by the offender as presenting a real risk to getting caught, either in the moment or post hoc, it might dissuade them from committing a crime at that particular time in that particular location.

But many offenders, including commercial robbers, report that CCTV is not difficult to circumvent (Gill, 2000), often by simply wearing a disguise. As Anthony (38) attested, 'CCTV is not really a deterrent, you can work around it, it's just, you know, a bit more of a pain in the arse.' The use of masks, balaclavas, hats, and glasses were commonly worn to avoid being identified by CCTV or by witnesses. For example, Tommy (24) explained that CCTV was inconsequential due to his disguise:

> I'd wear the hood, the balaclava rolled up, put me head down, back-pack on, gloves on in the pocket. I'd get, you know, 20, 30 metres away; I'd pull the balaclava down and run in. It's like the cameras are blocked out of me head; it's like I don't even know they're there. I don't think

> the paranoid thought: 'Oh, a camera's there, I'm not running in here.' Like, they're not going to stop me. It's only filming; you know what I mean?

For Tommy the cameras offered little deterrence because they could not intervene or stop him from committing the crime.

Josh (29) would wear stolen clothes when doing a robbery: 'Usually it'd be like a random person or something, like, I'd go jump a fence and pinch a pair of pants and a T-shirt off the line.' He'd then wear these over his usual clothing so that he had two layers. Upon leaving the scene of the robbery, he would remove the top layer and discard them so that he would no longer match the description of the suspect:

> sometimes I'll just run, take everything off and throw it in someone's bin and then, you know, just keep walking normally. So if you do get pulled up—if the police pull over, you've already got rid of all the clothes and you can just keep walking normally.

Kimsan (39) took a similar approach:

> Mate, you have to wear a balaclava, but you don't put the balaclava on straight away. You exit the car with it on your head so it looks like a hat and put your glasses on or whatever. You got to have a disguise. Like, say if I had long hair, I'd have a ponytail there and put that into my balaclava. So then I look like I've got short hair, with glasses on. And then, when you go out the back, take this and that off, jump in the car or whatever, um, drive off, then you have to burn everything.

CK also described the importance of looking natural while at the same time managing to avoid the CCTV cameras:

> You can't walk up the street dressed in black and have an AK47, you know. You might be walking up the street with a nice hat on, with a set of sunglasses on, and you might get right to the target like that or have a towel around yourself with a squash racket hanging out. You know, the towel's there and you're wiping your face and they haven't got you [on camera]. You've got to cover your face. You've got to find a way to cover your face.

Ben (19) was also cautious about being caught on CCTV while undertaking reconnaissance exercises. He explained that after finding a suitable target by visiting it a few times he would wait a minimum of eight weeks before robbing it to ensure that all of the CCTV recordings had been wiped.

It wasn't just visual footage that the armed robbers were concerned about; some were worried about leaving traces of DNA at the scene that could identify them at a later date. Maru (30) said that he would shave his arms and hands to avoid leaving any hairs at the scene. Josh (29) did the same, but additionally would wear a forensic suit under his regular clothes to avoid leaving any traces of skin or sweat at the scene.

> If I did use my own T-shirt—like, I think, once I've used my own T-shirt—and I'd just wear, like, the forensic suit underneath and then put my shirt over the top of that; or just use the overalls—the forensic little paper-thin overalls—and just put them on, so you know you're not going to drop any hair or—you know. So—I'm just worried about all the DNA and stuff like that, I guess, and—I mean, I don't have much hair on my body anyway, because I shave my arms and legs; but I still worry that you might, you know, drop a little bit of skin, anything, you know. And, like, because you're sweating, you know, you know—like, you know, the adrenaline kicks in when you're, you know, just about to walk in. So, you know—you just don't want to take that chance.

Indelible dye packs

Invented in the 1960s, dye packs were introduced in an attempt to prevent robbers from being able to spend stolen money and increase the chances of perpetrators being caught. Dye packs are made up of a stack of fake bank notes with a hollowed-out centre in which a radio-controlled incendiary device is placed. The pack is kept in the cashier drawer on a magnetic safety plate that prevents it from being activated. In a robbery situation, the dye pack is handed to the robber and the broken connection with the magnet plate preactivates it. There is a radio transmitter located near the exit of the premises, and when the device passes through it a timer is triggered that sets off the device after an elapsed period, usually 30–40 seconds. The pressurized canister inside the device produces a billowing cloud of red dye that stains everything that it comes into contact with including clothes, skin, and the real money.

Although Billy described them as 'a bit of a cunt' for him they would not deter a robbery, but rather just make the process of cleaning the money a little more arduous. He claims that he would undertake the relatively high-risk strategy of 'cleaning' it through the 'pokies' commonly found in RSL and other clubs.

BILLY: Like, if it [the dye pack] blows up, you know you've got to try and play it through the pokies to clean your money.

ET: That's how you do it?

BILLY: Yeah; always—always clean your money. So, if it's stolen from an armed robbery or if it's stolen from a burg or something, go and put it straight through the pokies or put it—put it on a bet or something, just to get your money back. Like, get it in different notes and that, so it's all different; it's all clean and that … I'd go and put it straight through the pokies, because I have a gambling addiction as well. So I'd—I'd gamble—I'd gamble—sometimes I'd gamble all of it. But then, you know, sometimes where you'd win triple what you had or—what I normally do is I just go and put it in and hit 'collect' and it comes out clean. And then you go and you get that exchanged into different notes, so it's all clean money.

Josh (29), having encountered the dye packs before, said he knew to look out for them:

> I guess if you know what you're looking for—if you've seen 'em before, you know. You know, like banks try and do it. You know, they'll put a big wad of 50-dollar notes on the counter and hope that you'll grab it, you know, because then you'll put it in your bag with the other money and run off and then it will explode. Being a drug addict and stuff like that, it's going to be hard to resist that big brick of, you know, 50-dollar notes or 100-dollar notes, but they're—they're useless. So, you know, if you're smart, you're not going to grab it; you're just going to leave it there; or, if you open the till, you know that, yeah, it will either be the top one, sitting on the top, or the one right at the bottom; so, when you take the last notes out, then it triggers it.

Police scanners

Several of the participants described how they tuned into police radios in order to keep abreast of any information that was being communicated about them. Mobile phone apps readily available to download from providers such as Google Play enable subscribers to listen to live audio from over 7,000 fire and police scanners, weather radios, amateur radio repeaters, air traffic, and marine radios from around the world. Max (23) described how useful it was tuning into the police radio network during and after committing crimes to see what information the police were communicating about the incident and if they were aware of his whereabouts:

> In Sydney and stuff, they use a digital police scanner and it's—it's harder to pick up on them. But, in country areas, they still use analogue, so it's easier. Like, when I drove around Ballowa,[6] I used to get pulled over and I used to plug it into the car stereo, and the copper would be in the car behind me and I'd be sitting there, listening to everything he's saying on the radio.

Max had repeatedly stabbed a man in the leg with a hunting knife after robbing him of his wallet (described in further detail in 'Blowing the lid: violence as a relief valve' in Chapter 8). He explained how he used the police scanner mobile phone app to listen for the police communicating information about the incident:

> [After the stabbing] I had to make my friend drive and I just—I laid in the back seat and just said straight away that, you know, 'This is going to come back and bite me in the arse.' I had the police scanner going on my phone—and, um, yeah, it was saying that he got taken to hospital for emergency surgery. And we stopped down the road and we were smoking ice and they [the police] said that the car we were in was last seen heading that way, so we took off. It's only, like, a two-second delay; two seconds after they start talking, I hear. Like, I was in bed in Ballowa, listening to them in Murralong still talking, saying that they were setting up spotlights for the crime scene and the fire brigade was coming to wash the blood away . . . I listened—like, mainly I was listening to the

[6] All local place names have been changed.

> scanner because I was worried that I'd already killed him, like. But, yeah, the whole time I was just—yeah, I knew I'd fucked up. I just knew because when I got out of the car, I dropped a set of keys out of my pocket and I thought in my head, 'On the way back, I'll grab 'em', but I forgot. And on the keys was a membership tag to Supercheap Auto that was registered in my mate's name, and then they tapped his phone and then ... it just all come undone.

It was Max's desire to remain fully informed of the situation that led to his conviction, as he explained in the following exchange:

MAX: I got—I got, um, stopped at the airport, trying to go over to Croatia the next day. Customs stopped me and took a download of my phone because, half an hour after the stabbing, I started searching it on Google, just thinking, like, maybe, like, I killed him or something was wrong. And then they downloaded it and used it in my brief: 'Why is he searching it half an hour after the stabbing before anyone even knew about it?' So, um, I was typing in 'Murralong robbery' and 'Murralong stabbing'.

ET: Did anything come up?

MAX: Nah; not till the next morning. But I continued listening to the scanner.

Max asserted that his motivation for listening to the scanner and 'Googling' to see if any information had been posted about the crime on the internet was a concern that he might have killed his victim. I couldn't help but wonder if, in fact, he derived some secondary pleasure from the attention his violent actions generated from the police and other emergency services. Being able to listen in to the police trying to locate him and scrambling efforts to track him down fuelled a narcissistic self-adulation.

When things go wrong

A much-fabled tale circulates frequently among armed robbers: a young man had spotted a bank in a sleepy town with lackadaisical security procedures that was a sure bet for an easy score and a quick getaway. The next day, wearing a balaclava and armed with a sawn-off shot gun, the man storms into the bank. The cashiers and customers freeze, awaiting the robber's next move:

'Put your hands up, motherstickers, this is a fuck up,' he shouts.

Deadly silence. The customers look at him and then look at each other, confused by what they had just heard. Then slowly, one by one, they start to laugh.

This story was relayed to me several times during the study—some telling it with gusto, embellishing it with additional details about the robber and his life, and heartily chuckling at his misfortune: 'a fuck up! Can you imagine?' In other tellings, it was not a humorous story, but rather a sombre account of how easily things can go wrong. For those offenders who use violent crime in part as a vehicle to assert their masculine supremacy, the prospect of being humiliated and laughed at was a fate worse than death.

In one of the very few studies to consider what happens when a robbery, or other crime, is unsuccessful, Nassauer (2018) analysed the CCTV video footage from 20 successful and failed robberies in the USA between 2010 and 2016. She concluded that 'successful store robberies follow specific situational rituals in which actors display adequate behaviors and emotions'. These 'rituals are broken if perpetrators or victims act out of character and display, even unintentionally, unexpected behaviors or emotions' (p. 125), much like the fate that befell the tongue-tied offender above.

Matt (27) recounted another story of accidental slippage in the performance of robbery. He had been drinking Turkish raki, which he said gave him the 'Dutch courage' to commit a robbery, but which would prove to be, quite literally, his downfall. Having stumbled into a service station, he pointed a machete at the cashier and demanded that he fill a bag with cash and another one with cigarettes. He recalls how he watched the cashier's hands shaking as he filled the bags, keeping a close eye on the machete that Matt was waving around. Pleased with his haul of '500-and-something dollars' and '91 packets of cigarettes', Matt turned to walk out of the store and head back to his apartment to continue his binge drinking. 'As I went to leave,' he tells me with a wince, 'I fell flat on my face. I just tripped over, you know. How embarrassing is that?' Not surprisingly, he was caught.

Conclusion

Despite what some perceive as the relative simplicity and ease of commercial armed robbery compared to other crime types, the potential for success is extremely precarious. Even the most meticulously planned robberies can, and do, go wrong due to unexpected events or the intervention of the much detested 'wannabe heroes'. We see a distinction between the professionals and amateurs, and observe that the shift in target selection in recent years—from banks to convenience stores, fast food outlets, and service stations—has left exposed the more impulsive and viscerally compelled armed robber. The robbers outlined the immediate security concerns and their attempts to negotiate them, using a range of techniques such as disguises, shaving body hair, and using mobile phone apps to listen in on police scanners.

PART THREE
REWARDS

7
The Usual Suspects
Money and Drugs

> I want a car now. I want this now. I want everything now. I don't want to wait six months for that or 12 months for this; I want it now. That's the mindset. Do you know what I mean? The instant gratification: bang, bang; that thing; bang, bang; this thing: I want it now.
>
> **(Robert, 51, reflecting back on his life)**

> We all want to sit around like fucking kings of the world.
>
> **(CK, 62)**

'If you didn't want the money, you wouldn't be doing it,' CK tells me. 'It's too heavy on the stress.' Although participants expressed multiple and complex, albeit interrelated, motivations for their offences, by far the most frequently articulated, and predictable, was a desire for cash. More varied was what the money was wanted for. Some fantasized about a lavish lifestyle: staying in hotels, driving flash cars, impressing women, frequenting casinos, and generally throwing money around with abandon. Typically, these men craved large sums, and less frequently. Others had developed expensive drug addictions that needed servicing, and any money, no matter how little, was a welcome step closer to their next fix. Although for some, the amount of money achieved was very low, relative to their usual financial position, it was plenty to fund a day or two of drug-fuelled partying. Some robbers dreamt of treating their mum, if only as a means to justify their crime, whereas others immersed themselves in a self-orchestrated boom and bust, feast and famine, the money slipping through their fingers like sand so as to necessitate the next job.

Armed Robbers. Emmeline Taylor, Oxford University Press. © Emmeline Taylor 2022.
DOI: 10.1093/oso/9780198855132.003.0007

So while money and drugs are the overarching themes of this chapter, offenders were largely operating within a broader commitment to what was often referred to enigmatically as 'the lifestyle': a culture that celebrated transgressive acts, gambling, excessive alcohol and drug use, overt consumerism, casual violence, disdain for deferred gratification, and a fast-living hedonistic lifestyle.

Versace and peanut butter: conspicuous consumption and crime

> Is your job boring and meaningless? Is your life empty? Consumption promises to fill the aching void
>
> **(Lasch, 1979: 72)**

The culture of consumption has become a definitive feature of advanced Western societies (Bauman, 1998; Lasch, 1979). As Hayward (2014: 3) describes it:

> the vast majority of people in the industrialised West now live in a world in which their everyday existence is, to a greater or lesser degree, dominated by the pervasive triad of advertising/marketing, the stylisation of social life, and mass consumption.

As the solid social structures that scaffolded modernity, such as the family and stable employment, have largely dissolved in what Zygmunt Bauman describes as 'liquid times', self-identity has become fluid and precarious. Ironically, at precisely the same time as there 'is a greater stress on creating one's identity, the building blocks of identity become less substantial' (Young, 2004). With the erosion of industrial labour and the shift in the traditional family set-up (see Chapter 4), new means of constructing masculine identity have emerged, based on conspicuous consumption. In *The Culture of Narcissism*, Christopher Lasch (1979) outlines how, in the modern age, consumption has come to be viewed 'as the answer to the age-old discontents of loneliness, sickness, weariness, [and] lack of sexual satisfaction'. A heightened emphasis on immediacy, expression, and exhilaration prevails in the consumer society as, to quote Albert Camus in *The Rebel*, 'Everyone tries to make his life a work of art.'

Writing in the late 1800s, the American sociologist, Thorstein Veblen, developed the notion of 'conspicuous consumption' to describe the acquisition of goods or use of services at a standard or quantity beyond what is necessary in practical terms. For example, driving a luxury car has little practical advantage in terms of transportation over an economy vehicle, but is purchased rather for its honorific value—that is, as a visible indicator of superior wealth and prestige. The culture of consumerism promotes the belief that self-worth can be achieved through the accumulation and overt display of consumer products. In order to bolster one's status such goods must be superfluous: 'no merit would accrue from the consumption of the bare necessaries of life' (Veblen, 1899: 96).

Conspicuous consumption can be applied to all categories of goods, from, in CK's case, peanut butter to Versace:

> Oh, hi-ho!—you know, $25,000 shopping sprees. You know, Saturday morning, just whatever you want, you know? Versace: my 10-year-old daughter would walk into Versace—and they're all on commission there—10 years old, and all the salespeople would run over and say, 'Hello, Lillian'—they knew her name. She's going to buy whatever she wants. My family are brand names—brand name everything, brand name peanut butter, yeah. The kids didn't know; they just knew we were rich.

The majority of participants in the study were strongly invested in consumerism, evidenced by the central role that the quest for 'the lifestyle' played in their narratives, typically comprised of money, drugs, commodities, and sex. Some, such as CK, appeared to go beyond this to display traits of what Lasch (1979) describes as a 'consumption-oriented narcissism'. As defined by Cisek et al. (2014):

> Narcissists are characterized by exhibitionism and vanity, and they see themselves as superior and entitled. To validate their grandiose self-image, narcissists purchase high-prestige products (i.e., luxurious, exclusive, flashy), show greater interest in the symbolic than utilitarian value of products, and distinguish themselves positively from others via their materialistic possessions.

Denied the legitimate means to acquire significant wealth, it is easy to see how this could quickly spill over into criminal activities, particularly when one has been acculturated to substantial affluence as a child, as CK was.

Stevo (29) was similarly seduced by the trappings of conspicuous consumption and began committing armed robberies, sometimes at a rate of five a week, in his teens. 'I love shopping!' he declared, and went on to describe frequenting the shopping mall to buy shoes.

> Back then, I didn't touch drugs; I didn't even like drugs. I smoked pot every now and then, but I've never been—like, I never liked drugs really. For me, it was shopping; I love shopping! Like, when they got me for the five armed robberies when I was 16—they got me, um, in Westfields going—they—they reckon that I spent 110 grand in seven days at Foot Locker. That's what they reckoned, but I don't know. I don't know, man. I just—shoes: shoes are my favourite things; they're—they're my favourite, you know. I have heaps; heaps. But I always—like, I always give the boys—like, if I've got something one of the boys wants, I'll give it to him straight away, you know. Like, if they say, 'Fuck, those are nice shoes,' I go, 'Here, have 'em,' you know, yeah, and stuff like that.

Lotto life and the roulette wheel of robbery

'Sometimes you get a lot; sometimes you get shit,' Stevo reflected matter-of-factly, conjuring up an image of robbery as a kind of roulette wheel for the more reckless down and outs. Similarly, Jack (37) thought of it as a kind of 'lucky dip'. Of course, monetary gain featured highly in the self-reported reasons for committing armed robbery among the cohort of offenders, and for some the rewards could be substantial. Jez (49) said anything less than 'a few hundred thousand' wasn't worth the effort, and CK put his expected haul in the millions. The robbery of the betting shop described by Sammy ('Learning the ropes', Chapter 5) yielded $33,000, rather a lot for a 12-year-old (although it was split three ways); and Liam (31) reported getting 'seven or eight thousand' dollars (split between two). Often the rewards for amateur opportunistic offences that involve little planning are low: typically, the non-professional armed robber will simply 'take whatever's in the till and three bottles—whatever you can carry—and out you go. It's not a lot . . .' (Chris, 36). Billy (20) was succinct in describing what he looked to get out of a 'rob': 'cash and grog and smokes'; but, relative to their usual financial position, these offenders could still feel like 'high-rolling big shots for a few days' (Baumeister 2001: 110).

Josh, aged 29 at the time of interview, was serving seven years, having committed 'probably four or five' hold-ups; he described the allure of quick and easy cash as his motivating factor:

> Money. It was fast money, like easy... You don't have to sell merchandise or, you know?... It's really all about the money, you want to get as much as you can. You don't want to walk in there and get 200 bucks or something, you know.

Similarly, Ben (19) pursued armed robbery for 'money, heaps of money' and had set his acceptable threshold as 'a minimum of two grand'. Other interviewees had particularly modest hopes, given the risks involved. For example, Jesse (22) was quite happy with the relatively low rewards that a liquor store rather than a bank might yield, even though this meant having to commit more frequent crimes:

> Some people say, 'Go out the back, get the money out of the safe', but I personally would never do that. [It's] too much stuffing around, you know? Like, I'd rather just—because I don't need that much money—I don't want $20,000 or $10,000; it'd be good, but I'm only after a thousand or two, maybe $500.

Kai (27) stated that he 'wasn't expecting nothing [anything]' from the robbery, but after just 49 seconds found himself with 'fifteen hundred dollars', 'bottles of liquor', and 'about eight cartons of smokes', and reported that he would have been pleased with that had he not been caught at the scene. Similarly, Cameron (27) said his first hold-up resulted in 'under a thousand' dollars; while he 'wasn't ecstatic' or 'over the moon', he was on the whole happy that he 'was a thousand dollars richer'.

The money was used, at least for the most part, to transcend the tedium of everyday life and enter a euphoric haze of excessive drug and alcohol use, partying, and/or conspicuous consumption. Typical purchases included clothes, cars, alcohol, and drugs, as well as gambling. Ben explained: 'First you got to get away from there [scene of the robbery], get out of the car and then, um, get rid of your clothes, count your money and, then party!'. Billy (20) had similar objectives:

ET: What do you do straight afterwards?

BILLY: Go get on [score drugs] and then go back to my place, charge up for a bit, and then go out and do the same thing that night.

ET: So 'charge up': is that—

BILLY: Get on the ice and get drunk.

Alluding to the carnivalesque and hedonic spoils of crime, on the rare occasion that a substantial amount of money was acquired, several of the robbers in this sample reported that it would be spent immediately, usually all of it in just a few days, typifying the pursuit of 'earning and burning money' (Katz, 1988: 215).

ET: How long would $17,000 last?

BILLY: A day. Two days at the most.

ET: Seriously?

BILLY: Yeah . . . I just can't help it; I can't help it. That's why I'm back out there doing it again that night.

Similarly, Tommy (27) was attracted to commercial robbery because of the immediacy of the rewards, which he would spend as quickly as he could:

> I once spent $16,000 in three days. I was just gambling, and drugs, like, for all the people hanging off me, like, frigging yeah. I—I had nothing to show for it. Like, I had clothes and shoes and that, but I had nothing at the end of it. I went back to my mate and he's going, 'What?'—'What? We're not doing another armed robbery'—like—'we just did one three days ago.' I'm going, 'Fucking'—'get the fuck up; let's go.'

After getting $20,000 from an armed robbery at the age of 17, Stevo—now aged 29—said he'd received a Facebook notification on his phone that it was his associate's birthday, prompting him to embark on a four-day partying binge.

> It was my co-ie's birthday, yeah . . . and I told him, 'Well, yeah, let's go.' So we went out, this and that, yeah. I took him—went to this hotel: girls, this and that, drugs and like, escorts and that; yeah, escorts, strippers. Then I was—it was just rack [cocaine]; rack and pot and then drinking. Like, we started on a Thursday and went till, like, Sunday or Monday—Monday. It

> was just fun, you know. Yeah; I—I was—I was off my head, yeah; yeah, we were off our heads. That's how we think of money; you don't hold on to it; you can't hold on to it. Fuck, what can you do, you know? Like, as fast as it comes, it goes, you know. You're spewing but, fuck, what can you do? You just go do it again, I guess.

Wright and Decker (1994: 36) argue that criminal behaviour often germinates following a period of 'intense self-indulgence', situating the offences of their participants in a commitment to a street culture that celebrates excessive alcohol and drug use, overt consumerism, casual violence, gambling, disdain for deferred gratification, and a fast-living hedonistic lifestyle—a far more nuanced and complex pathway to armed robbery than the rational and reasoning offenders depicted in other studies (for example, Feeney, 1986; Gill, 2000; Morrison and O'Donnell, 1996). Katz (1988: 198) explains how some 'stickup men' construct their lives so as to be dominated by action; taking a 'temporal form', episodic and cyclical, 'so that they can get into the action more or less spontaneously and with an air of indefinitely extended commitment'.

The men in the present study, similarly, set in motion a cycle whereby the profits of their offence would be almost immediately spent on 'partying', thus requiring further criminal activity just a few days later. This cyclical behaviour of boom and bust creates 'an environment of pressures that guide them back towards crime' (Katz 1988: 216). In a similar vein, Bauman (2013) argues that 'we prefer the hunt to the capture ... catching a hare is an anti-climax; it only makes more seductive the prospect of another hunt'.

In addition to the drugs and intense partying, such reckless consumption enables the procurement of 'masculine capital' (Mullins, 2006: 69). Nayak (2006: 813) suggests that 'by exhibiting "spectacular masculinities" of white male excess, young men accrue a body capital that has a currency and a local exchange within the circuits they inhabit'. At times, however, the 'intensity and grim determination' (Topalli and Wright, 2013: 43) that often characterize the post-stick-up partying slides into pure hedonic indulgence of such force, such reckless abandon, that it can exceed pleasurable boundaries and become self-destructive. Indeed, during this complete surrender of inhibitions, what Wright and Decker (1997) describe as 'desperate partying', more crimes are often committed.

Poverty and pecuniary emulation

> Some people think luxury is the opposite of poverty. It is not. It is the opposite of vulgarity.
>
> **(Coco Chanel)**

Robert tells me that he hasn't had a birthday since he was 16. There are many things that are different in jail, and one of them is that the passing of time is not always a cause for celebration. Although the ebbing away of days brought inmates closer to their release date, birthdays were too stark a reminder of years wasted and the insurmountable separation from the outside world. There were no cakes, no parties, no birthday cards for most incarcerated men. I knew from Robert's record that he was 51. Reluctantly he tells me that he turned 50 in prison, turned 40 in prison, and so on. It's little wonder he doesn't mark the occasion. Like Peter Pan, who also didn't have birthdays, Robert struck me as a boy who never grew up. Despite his ageing frame and wiry silver-grey hair, he had a childlike demeanour—timid, shy, and eager for praise.

Robert's story is distinctive, as he is one of just two participants (the other being Cameron) in this study who described his family as an inhibitor to his engagement in crime—there was no history of violence or emotional abuse, there was no drug addiction, and none of his relations had a criminal record. His first-ever offence was a break and enter at the age of 10. It was a

> boring Sunday afternoon and there was this big house in the area that stood out. I was an inquisitive kid. It was a bit of an adventure—having to get past the dogs, climbing up through the roof. I didn't want to take anything. It wasn't for the 'earn' back in those days.

After this initial dalliance with crime, it would be seven years until the next offence. Robert attributed this intermission to a desire not to upset his parents:

ROBERT: This is going to sound crazy to you—I always didn't want mum and dad to be ashamed of me or embarrassed. Like, you know, in those days, the police would grab you and you might be riding a motorcycle or up to what they thought was no good. So, you know, it's very embarrassing for your mother and father. So that was a factor. It was not out of goodness in me. I don't—I'm not saying I'm bad or anything, but the underlying factor was that I was more concerned how it reflected on mum and dad, in the main.

ET: So your parents were quite straight?

ROBERT: Yes, yeah, yeah, yeah. Honest; you know? That kind of 'honest as the day is long' sort of family. No grey areas; black and white, yeah, yeah.

Realizing as a teenager that his family were financially poor, although well off in many other respects, Robert began to yearn for an income to support a flash lifestyle, and his criminal activity escalated from the age of 17. He told me that shortly after training to be a boilermaker, he had a realization that he was always going to be poor, always working overtime to earn just enough money to pay the bills. He was earning $100 a week and suddenly the revelation came: 'If I did something wrong, I'd earn a year's wages, plus, in one hit'. Robert started committing armed robberies and was now serving eight years in prison. He told me he had lost count of how many hold-ups he had committed to fulfil his desire for money, mostly so that he could impress women. He revelled in buying expensive cocktails and exuding the confidence of an affluent businessman. He also wanted to treat his mum.

> You come to that stage in your life where you didn't even realize you grew up poor because, you know, you got the love of your parents, you've got food, you've got clothing. You actually think you're well off, until—until you get to a stage where you think, 'Shit, we were poor,' do you know what I mean? We were—we were poor. It's nice to have money because, well, it's an illusion that, well, you're not poor any more and you have all these grand plans—there's always part of you that'd like to kind of maybe spoil your mum. Like, my mum's Irish and I used to think, 'Oh, I'd love to send me mum back over to Ireland to have a big cruise or something like that.' Do you know what I mean? That's—that's the love for your mother, but it's a little bit of justifying too . . . It was the bravado, like, to impresses the girls—do you know what I mean—to go out, you know, and throw money around and, you know, like, tell the girls, like, 'Oh, yeah, we come from rich families,' or that you're a businessman, you know. Everyone wants a good time. If you earn $60 a day digging a hole for eight hours a day, you wouldn't be spending $20 on a cocktail drink for a lady. Do you know what I mean?

In his overview of conspicuous consumption, Veblen (1899: 70) noted how 'certain victuals, and more particularly certain beverages, are strictly reserved for the use of the superior class'. Such symbolic displays of status were beyond reach on a labourer's wage. Robert's desire to reject his working-class destiny and reinvent himself through conspicuous consumption was tangible. Simultaneously with Robert's awakening to his family's financial status came another realization—one that would prove to be far more life-changing: he realized that the only people he knew that were rich were committing crimes:

> the only people I saw with the ready money—like, money in their pocket—were blokes who I knew were up to 'things'. It might have been someone's older brother or someone and you just knew about it and, like, they were the ones that had the nice motorbike, the nicer car than your dad had, you know, the nice girlfriends.

Robert yearned for similar honorific displays of overt wealth to elevate his status, but understood that his training as a boilermaker was never going to provide the lifestyle he coveted.

> It's terrible not being a skilled person—do you know what I mean—where you have to—like, you know, it doesn't matter how hard you're going to work, you know—like, even a brickie's labourer: you can kill yourself working and you're going to be pulling, say, $1,100. Do you know what I mean? Like—and you know yourself you're killing yourself for that; where maybe, if you were someone skilled and earning, say, $1,500 to $1,800, you might think, 'Well, in a few weeks I can get that.' Do you know what I mean? There's nothing worse too when you get it—like, when you work and you think, 'Ooh, look at that bundle of money I got.' By the time you pay for this and pay for that, got to pay for petrol, got to buy food to get to work. I used to think to myself, 'Wow! How—how do they really do it?' Do you know what I mean? And I admire 'em; I—I—don't get me wrong: I do admire 'em for it; but I just think to meself, 'It's so hard.' Do you know what I mean?

It's only now, still incarcerated in his fifties, that Robert realizes that his reasoning was perhaps not so cogent after all. He has spent decades of his life behind bars; each time upon being released he'd get an overwhelming sense of needing to catch up—to own a car, to buy a house—but being an 'ex-con' with no skills and few prospects, it wouldn't be long before he was returned to jail for another bungled robbery.

CK, like Robert, was also something of an anomaly; but his background was the polar opposite. He had come from a very wealthy family, which, he explained, gave him both a distorted view of what money could do and an insatiable greed—a lethal combination. CK had once been a competitive show jumper and professional polo player. He told me in simple terms what had inspired him to commit robbery:

> Greed. I was brought up that money was everything; that money meant everything. I was brought up in a family, a wealthy family, and everything we got from my father. He was self-made, but we were quite rich; we had our own plane and stuff like that . . . We were wealthy; we were wealthy. I rode show jumpers to a professional level. I played grade polo . . . Money was everything. My father was flogging my mother, flogging me, but money fixed it; money fixed it. So I just thought that—I think that that probably gave me that—that—that greed, you know: that money's the—money's the solution. So I thought, 'Well, I'll get lots of money.'

It was through this greed that CK was tempted to reject his training as a plumber and begin a much more lucrative criminal career dealing drugs and robbing banks.

> I'm a licensed plumber. I worked intermittently until I was 26. When I finished my apprenticeship, I stopped working as a plumber. I was just—I was in—I worked for a big Mafia guy through the seventies. I moved to Bondi and I . . . got into the drug scene there but not as a drug addict. I took LSD and different things for excitement . . . it was very new and there was a lot of money in it. So I started doing small—like, I'd—I'd buy trips for 50c and sell 'em for $4 and stuff like that and I'd do a few hundred but not much; but it was much more money than plumbing. And then I was [horse] riding—I was riding a lot then too, like, show jumpers, although I was sponsored at that time—I was riding for a couple of big sponsors—but I was making much, much more money just selling these trips. So that sort of led me into really understanding that there was money in crime. And then as a result of being involved in that, I met a lot of people that were sort of underworld type people. And then, as a result—I was always reliable and good at what I did so that I just moved up through the grades.

It was clear that CK was never going to be content with an average income and an average life. His upbringing had been exceptionally affluent and he had been exposed to well-connected players in organized crime from an early age. I wondered, however, whether the men from more modest backgrounds could ever feel satisfied working an average job for an average income after experiencing the lavish lifestyle that the profits of armed robbery could provide, even if the illicit highs only lasted a few days.

Stevo (29), more than most, seemed to have been caught up in the 'lotto life' of armed robbery since being a young teenager—the instant gratification and the boom and bust it provided. I was interested to know whether he could ever entertain a more conventional life.

ET: Can you ever see a way of having a job and just using your wages to go shopping and buy stuff?

STEVO: Yeah; yeah, I can. It'd have to be a good job, but. Like, I—I wouldn't—oh, don't get me wrong; I'll still—like, I work; I work and that.

ET: What do you work doing?

STEVO: Well, I was doing scaffolding when I was out, but I did anything, you know: scaffolding, warehousing. Any of that stuff—you know, I'll do it. But it's just, um, like, I'll still be doing something on the side, you know.

ET: So it could never be enough?

STEVO: Yeah, pretty much. Like, I don't know; maybe; maybe. It'll take a lot, but—but, yeah, maybe.

ET: What do you think would make you happy? When you think of being happy, is it about having money and clothes and women and drugs? What do you want?

STEVO: Yeah, pretty much. Yeah, just—I want—just being able to do whatever you want whenever you want. Like, that's it pretty much really. Like, just being able to, like, just do anything you want whenever you want, just—like, 'Oh, yeah, we'll go here; yeah, we'll get a VIP booth at Marque;[1] we'll do this; we'll do that,' you know—like, anything. Like, anything; like—like, just whatever you want, you know. Like, whatever you want, you can do it. There's no—when you got money—when you can do that, fuck, you're laughing, you know.

[1] Marque was a famous restaurant in Surrey Hills, Sydney, awarded three 'hats' by *The Good Food Guide* in 2004 and named '2010 breakthrough restaurant' in the World's 50 Best Restaurants. It closed in 2016.

ET: How do you feel about being in prison then? If the thing that makes you happy is being able to do whatever you want whenever you want, I guess being in prison does not really allow you to do that.

STEVO: Yeah; but that's the risk that—that—that—that we take, you know, and that's what—like, I've come to terms with it. Like, you want to play games, so this is what happens, you know. So what can you do? You just got to roll with it, you know.

It was curious, given Stevo's emphasis on transcending the limitations that his social positioning imposed, in order to be able 'do anything you want whenever you want', that this would ultimately lead to the exact opposite: being denied liberty and incarcerated in a concrete cell for years on end. It seemed like a Faustian exchange.

Drugs

Not surprisingly, in addition to the desire for cash, drugs and alcohol featured heavily in the self-reported motivating factors of robbers. Matthews' (2002) research in England found that the relationship between drugs and armed robbery takes two major forms: in some cases the need to get money to buy drugs underscores the motivation for the offence, whereas, in others, the offender's intoxication disinhibits them to the extent that they commit the crime. In my study, this second group was found to be further divided into those who had decided to commit the robbery beforehand and used drugs or alcohol to boost their confidence or calm their nerves (see also Chapter 5), and those who had taken drugs and claimed that it was only once they were under the influence that the impetus to commit a robbery materialized. In separating out these two categories, it is recognized that knowing one has the potential to commit violent offences having taken drugs muddies cause and effect.

Individuals who reported committing armed robbery to buy drugs invariably described their situation as 'desperate'. This desperation often accrued as part of a broader set of highly aroused emotions, including anger and fear, that influence judgement and decision making (Topalli and Wright, 2013). Typically, offenders in the present study would be starting to withdraw from drugs—'hanging out'—and would become increasingly frantic about generating the cash for their next hit.

Billy (20) smoked crack, to which he ascribed some causality for his offences:

> If I never started smoking crack, I probably would have never done a crime in my life. But, you know, you start smoking, you pick up an addiction and then you need to feed that addiction ... If you're hanging out for it, that's when you think, 'I've got to do this so I can get on,' you know? Like you give yourself no other alternative; there's no other choice so you have to do it. You're pretty well telling yourself you have to do it.

Josh (29) told me that being in a state of withdrawal was the most dangerous time to do a robbery:

> If you were high at the time you might, you know, let the gun off or whatever and then if they still don't hand over the money you might think, 'I'll go somewhere else' and walk out. But if you're in withdrawal, you're going to do damage to get that money. You're not leaving that shop without the money.

Most of the drug-affected offenders in the sample were using methamphetamine, referred to colloquially as 'ice'. Jayden (25) described commercial robbery as a 'junkies' crime' with the cognitive process limited to 'I've got no money; I need to get a fix; I'm going to rob a servo straightaway.' Other respondents agreed:

> If you go on ice every day, you just become desperate for it 'til the day you'll do something like that.
>
> **(Murray, 32)**

> Well, with the ice, because it costs so much and it takes you out of the normal normalness, like, inside your head. You think crazy thoughts and that. So I started to look for more money.
>
> **(Jesse, 22)**

Kenny (56) was one of only three interviewees who admitted to being a heroin user; he attributed his armed robbery to 'total desperation' for drugs. Another was Nick, 37, who had 'hit the heroin' after splitting up with his wife. He claims his one and only criminal offence was the armed robbery he was in prison for at the time of interview, and explains that drugs were the causal factor:

> I was waiting for my dealer and I was hanging out [withdrawing] and one of my mates said to me, 'Fucking take a few of these pills,' and I took a handful of pills. Yeah, I was smashed off my face on Xanax and went and did an armed robbery . . . I didn't know until my mates told me that night that I actually did it.

Although Nick acknowledges that he committed the offence, he clearly apportions blame to the drugs he had taken, and furthermore assigns responsibility for his having taken them to one of his acquaintances. Similarly, Josh (29) reasons that funding a heroin addiction gave him a 'drive' to commit robbery, claiming, 'there's no way I would have done it if I wasn't on drugs. Like, I'm just not that sort of person, but the drugs just gave me that drive, I guess.'

Matt (27) had 'a bit of a problem with drink' and engaged in binge-offending whenever he'd been on 'a big spirits bender', typically holding up several premises in one episode and just a few minutes apart. In just one evening, after four days drinking neat rum with tequila chasers, he robbed three service stations and a restaurant in quick succession. His alcohol-fuelled crime spree only came to an end that night when he ended up in hospital having put his hand through a glass window. He was convicted of all four robberies. In a similar way, Ben (19) outlined how excessive alcohol impaired his decision making and resulted in him doing 'silly things' like armed robbery:

> I reckon robbery's a stupid, silly thing to do but when I drink, I think stupid and silly things are good to do . . . you don't even know if there's money there or not, and, um, you could get hurt; a person could hurt you or you could hurt someone and the police take it very seriously.

Most people, having imbibed too much alcohol, have done something that could be regarded as a bit silly—thinking karaoke is a good idea and missing the last bus home frequently feature in my own repertoire—but regarding armed robbery as a 'silly' outcome of drinking too much is something of an understatement; the police do indeed take it very seriously. In all of the above accounts, the offenders dissociate themselves from their crimes by claiming that it is not really in their character.

The robberies committed by the drug-affected individuals in this study were largely impulsive, chaotic, involved very little, if any, planning, and resulted in comparatively low yields. Problematizing the rationality doctrine, it can also be temporal: what can appear to be a rational decision at one moment becomes illogical the next. As Matt (27) reported, contrary to the common after-the-fact rationalizations in offender interviews, he experienced the inverse. He was serving four years' custody followed by two years' parole for six armed robberies. He explained that all of the robberies he had committed 'were for different reasons', but that 'it's nothing that really makes sense, if you know what I mean? Like, at the time they made sense; but when you sober up and look back, you think "you idiot"'.

Conclusion

A culture of consumerism, permeating all levels of society, instilled in many of the men in this study an insatiable desire for the appurtenances of consumer culture—fashion, fast cars, luxury hotels, and lavish leisure pursuits—but all were too aware that their chances of achieving them by legitimate means were slim, if not non-existent. Their financial rewards were hugely varied, ranging from hundreds of thousands of dollars to nothing. The majority of offenders reported gaining in the region of \$500–\$5,000, but for most this fairly modest return was enough to fund a day or two of excessive drinking, drugs, gambling, staying in hotels, and soliciting sex workers. Thus, while financial reward certainly featured in the motivations for armed robbery, it appears to be just part of the picture. The non-utilitarianism of many offences suggests that other factors are woven into their aetiology, explored in further detail in the next chapter.

8
The Magic Carpet Ride
Flow, Affect, and Automaticity

> I like working at the edge of thinking.
>
> **(CK, 62)**

The previous chapter highlighted the ways in which broad social and cultural conditions, entangled with the desire for quick cash and the accoutrements of wealth, can provide vital clues to the motivations underlying armed robbery. The proceeds of robbery can fund wild spending sprees on hedonistic pursuits including drugs, alcohol, sex, and gambling, during which time the reality of an otherwise humdrum life could be temporarily suspended. The offender is transported to a parallel world where they are high-rolling big shots—anything is possible, if only for a few days or hours. Although money was the overall driving factor, some offenders experienced multifaceted circumstances that led to the decision to commit commercial armed robbery. For many of these men, armed robbery, particularly when well executed, provided a currency of its own, delivering things of value that money simply cannot buy. As Chris (36) reflected, 'You've gotta think why not do a burglary? [Why not] plan to go back after-hours and ram raid and steal as much alcohol as you can and as many smokes as you can?'

Chris's rhetorical questions reveal that there are other contributory factors to the decision to be an armed robber, since other types of crime could provide greater financial return for, in all likelihood, less risk. Several studies have attested, particularly those falling under the banner of cultural criminology, that those engaging in criminal behaviour are often fulfilling needs and ambitions through their criminal activity, consciously or subconsciously, beyond monetary gain; a desire to exact revenge, derive pleasure, gain control, lose control, or elevate status among peers are also common

Armed Robbers. Emmeline Taylor, Oxford University Press. © Emmeline Taylor 2022.
DOI: 10.1093/oso/9780198855132.003.0008

motivations (Hobbs, 2013; Katz, 1988; Presdee, 2000; Taylor, 2017b). To impose a limited and homogenous assumption that all criminal stimulus is financially driven is to ignore 'the very essence of much everyday criminality: pleasure, excitement, anger, and risk' (Ferrel, 2007: 3–4). Despite recurrent calls to be more attuned to the affective aspects of criminal behaviour, extant conceptual models within criminology are severely limited, and ones that move beyond synonymizing affect with emotion almost entirely absent. This chapter seeks to explore some of the affective qualities of robbery, particularly the visceral and felt dimensions, in a bid to remediate some of the enduring deficits in the understanding of contemporary criminal behaviour.

Boredom and buzzes: the criminal high

It has been shown that many violent acts may be enjoyable for those committing them, not due to sadistic tendencies, but rather many perpetrators, particularly undersocialized males, seek out thrills and excitement to counter a sense that most of life is tedious and dull (Forsyth and Marckese 1993; Larkin 1979; Pfefferbaum and Wood 1994). Apter (1992) has described the seductive appeal of risky behaviour as an escape from boredom, and the alleviation of the mundane realities of everyday life. Reflecting this, Billy (20) shrugged off armed robbery as just 'something to do'. Similarly, Liam (31) described his pathway into crime, committing his first hold-up at the age of 12 to alleviate the boredom he associated with long days just kicking about with friends: 'It started off out of boredom, you know, not going to school or anything. So it was just that, all day, boredom and, you know, money, grog ...'

Poor or non-existent school attendance, followed by the ennui of low-paid routine employment—or long stints of unemployment, as was often the case—characterized the lives of many of these men. The days merged into one continuous blur, punctuated only by the highs of illicit drug taking or numbed by excessive alcohol use. The absence of sensory stimulation propagated a thirst for hedonic pleasures satiated only by the extremes of criminal activity. Baumeister and Campbell (1999) recognize that 'acts of violence and aggression can provide such thrills, and therefore, in an important sense, evil acts can be fun'. In this way, armed robbery offers 'the criminal an opportunity for a passionate, intensely authentic experience' (Lyng, 2004: 361).

Reference to 'adrenaline' was common throughout the interviews, and it was apparent that the word was used to capture a specific corporeal feeling that was perhaps ineffable to those who had not experienced it. Tommy (27) described it as being similar to the high attained from extreme sports such as skydiving, or like smoking methamphetamine, but 'a hundred times better':

> Have you ever been skydiving or anything like that, bungee jumping? If you do stickups, it's the same, but it's, like, a hundred times better. It's euphoric—you feel good, you know? You just get a huge surge of adrenaline. Like, the drugs and that: the drugs give you similar, but it's synthetic, like. They're not as good—the drugs aren't as good as that feeling, mm. It's very addictive; yeah. Like, you want that feeling every day. Like, I'll go and buy, like, an ounce of ice and sit there and smoke it and smoke it and smoke it, but I'll never get that same feeling. Even talking about it now I still get, like, a little bit tingly and that. I try not to think about it, because then it'll be hard to leave it behind, you know, because it's a good feeling. Like, there's other ways—like—I met other blokes who do big armed robs and they were saying, like, between jobs and that, they're, like, skydiving or they'll just go for a mad drive; like, they'll just pump it as fast as they can go, you know, to try and get that adrenaline, you know?

Some of the same vernacular was used to describe the activities of skydiving, driving fast cars, and committing armed robberies. For example, Tommy articulates how a driver would 'pump it' to go faster, while Stevo (29) referred to robberies as pumping: 'You know if the last robbery went good then sometimes you won't need to pump for a while, but sometimes you just—you want to pump it, you know.' Will (41) described the immediate heightened sensory feelings after a successful robbery:

> Oh, you got the adrenaline pumping; that's for sure. You know, you've got away with it and you're just thinking, 'Fuck, I've got all this money'—you know—'Fuck, what am I going to do?' Nine times out of ten, we didn't know what we were going to do with the money, you know, so we just—we'd go and buy a carton of beer and just have a drink in a park and sit around and talk about either what we were going to do next or where we're going to do the next robbery.

Kimsan (39) explained that some armed robbers were thrill seeking:

> Well, you know how you got thrill seekers that jump off a plane and, ah—this is their way. They—they might be good at it—like, doing their stunts and whatever—but the people that do armed rob: they—they are good at what they do and they get a—a—yeah, that's how the human mind works, you know. If you're good at something and you get a rush out of it, you're going to automatically do it.

The language used to describe the ostensibly very different behaviours of reckless driving, skydiving, and robbing directly evokes imagery of injecting adrenaline into an otherwise flat state of being. Attempting to counter a mundane lifestyle characterized by boredom, the banality of unemployment, and a lack of prospects, armed robbery—and other extremes—delivered a hit. The structural and geographic inequities that delivered many of the men into relative poverty also delimited their access to the means of escape:

> As a consequence of the inequality of resources in society, some of the ways of transcending mundane life are more open to some groups of people than others. Skydiving, for example, may offer a transcendent experience but is unlikely to be available to many young black members of the urban underclass. Crack on the other hand, may provide a similarly transcending experience, but unlike skydiving is available to all, rich and poor.
>
> **(O'Malley and Mugford, 1994: 209)**

For some, the high delivered by an armed robbery was so seductive that they immediately craved the sensation again, as Matt (27) elucidates:

> The person I was with was just driving past and I said, 'pull in here,' and I did that robbery, and then got a big buzz out of it and so then drove down the street and did another one four minutes later ... And about an hour later, I robbed another servo.

Hayward (2007) claims that crime should be understood as the 'existential pursuit of passion and excitement'—a desperate attempt to escape the humdrum realities and banalities of 'regular' life. Since undergoing counselling and engaging with a drug-rehabilitation programme, David (34) had become reflective about the motivations for the robberies that he had committed. He had had a difficult relationship with his mother and experienced an abusive childhood, which led to him living on the streets from the age of 11. I asked him what motivated the robberies he had committed. After a thoughtful pause, he replied:

> Um, probably a few years ago, I would have told you 'just money'. But, since I done this drug program, they sort of—I've never done counselling before, so there's a lot of one-on-one counselling and they really, like, dissect you. Talking with the psychs and that, there was a part—there's a side of me that enjoyed doing it. It wasn't about the money. I really enjoyed it. I've taken drugs a lot but that's a different kind of rush, a different feeling. And it's not about controlling other people; it's more about, you know, 'This is'—I don't know, um—'this is fucked up, but I sort of enjoy it.'

David went on to describe the kick he would get from seeing people watching his offences reported on the news, oblivious that he—the perpetrator—was among them:

> Like, at one of the stickups, after one of our armed robberies, I was at a hotel and I left on my own and I had a drink by myself—just doing little fucking things like I had a slap on the pokies and the person behind the bar give me my drink and the news was pumping it, the news was pumping what had happened, and I was just real casual and I said, 'Fuck'—like—'that's pretty bad', like—but I knew—and me knowing, like, what'd happened there, I had it first-hand; *I was there.* And then that person was like, 'Yeah, that's really bad,' and they're like—they have no idea that I've got money that's from *that* robbery paying for that drink.

The pleasure elicited from both the attention the media gave his crimes and the elevated superiority he felt by being the orchestrator of the incident provided a similar narcissistic relish to that which Max experienced when hearing about his own crimes via the police scanner (Chapter 6). The newsworthiness of the offence appeared, for David, to elevate him from a 'nobody' to someone who commanded coverage on the television and people talking about him in a hotel bar. Tommy (27) also enjoyed the notoriety that committing armed robberies provided. He would take photographs on his mobile phone of the money that he stole and 'screen shots' of any online news coverage to look through at a later date, no doubt reliving some of his crimes.

> I had heaps of photos in my phone: every robbery, guns—everything—stacks of money. Like, I wasn't thinking right. I thought I was infamous. I thought I was cool, you know. 'Far out, yeah, look at all that money and that,' or, 'Look at that, my gun.' Like, every single robbery I ever done: I screen shotted the frigging thing and I had 'em in my phone. Like, the police destroyed the phone, the idiots. If they had have just looked in the photos, far out, I was gone. Even if they just took the SD card and looked in the photos file, I'd be finished. I'd looked at the news clips and screen shotted the thing. Like, how stupid! But I thought I was cool, you know—infamous, you know. I'd look through them all the time—like, look at all the—all my robberies and that and go, 'Yeah, I'm infamous'—like, 'I'm like Ned Kelly.'

On the edge of thinking: in and out of control

Inspired by Hunter S. Thompson's term 'edge-work' in *Fear and Loathing in Las Vegas*, Stephen Lyng has developed a sociology of risk-taking. The resulting dehyphenated concept of 'edgework' describes the voluntary pursuit of risky behaviour in order to fulfil a need to order one's existence through excitement and thrills. This perspective explains how individuals derive intense sensual experiences from high-risk pursuits. According to Lyng (1990: 859), edgeworkers possess:

> [T]he ability to maintain control over a situation that verges on complete chaos, a situation most people would regard as entirely uncontrollable. The more specific aptitudes required for this type of competence involve the ability to avoid being paralyzed by fear and the capacity to focus one's attention and actions on what is most crucial for survival.

A characteristic of edgework is that the 'individual typically feels a significant degree of fear during the initial, anticipatory phases of the experience ... But as one moves to the final phases of the experience, fear gives way to a sense of exhilaration and omnipotence' (Lyng 1990: 860).

Encapsulating this transitory phase from fear to exhilaration, Josh (29) described robbery as being 'intimidating, scary but an adrenaline rush at the same time'; similarly, Murray (32) said, 'My adrenaline was going really fast and my heart was going fast and things like that.' When asked what he thought of armed robbery, Sammy described being 'pumped up on adrenaline and fear'. David (34), using the analogy of a roller-coaster, described how the physiological arousal of fear could be harnessed and turned into something exhilarating: 'you can channel that fear into something better, into good energy, and it's more, um, sort of, "Fuck, this is off its head," but it's like, you know, maybe a roller-coaster's fucking going crazy and—I hate roller-coasters.'

Negotiating the boundary between chaos and control might not only provide an intense sensual experience, but also an opportunity to exert power and control in lives that otherwise are largely passive and inert. Leith and Baumeister (1996: 1250) explain how unpleasant emotional states can initiate such self-defeating and risky behaviours:

> [N]egative affect causes people to make choices in a way that leads to nonoptimal courses of action: Specifically, one that may indeed hold out the chance of some highly positive outcome but also carries substantial risks or costs. More precisely, when people are upset, they tend to choose high-risk, high-payoff options.

Armed robbery delivered the sensory surge craved by these men to counter their otherwise bleak everyday life in a 'bulimic' society, 'that choruses the liberal mantra of liberty, equality and fraternity yet systematically in the job market, on the streets, in the day-to-day contacts with the outside world, practises exclusion' (Young 2003: 395).

Automaticity and flow: the magic carpet ride

A recurrent theme among the armed robbers in this study was the way in which they believed the enactment of robbery could cause them to transcend the ordinary limitations and constraints of time, awareness, and ability. For some, voluntarily placing themselves in situations of such extreme danger and fear enabled them to ascend into a different mental state, one similar to the 'flow state' first identified in academic terms by the psychologist Mihaly Csikszentmihalyi. In his book *Flow: The Psychology of Optimal Experience* (1990), Csikszentmihalyi characterizes this state as being when an individual becomes so immersed in an activity that they develop a heightened sense of ability and control, feel automaticity in their actions and responses, lose self-consciousness, and experience a shift in their perception of time. The flow state is often referred to colloquially as 'being in the zone'.

CK (62) described robbery as like stepping on to 'a magic carpet' and outlined how it produced a state of heightened sensory awareness:

> Once you step over the point of no return; it's like you just jump on a magic carpet because everything—you've already foreseen it so you don't really think it. All you do is you just—whoooosh [*makes swirling movement with his hand*]. Everything is—if—if I was looking at you and a car went past behind my back, I'd say, 'Red Commodore, four people.' It's amazing—all the—all the senses start really operating—you know, peripheral, everything. Nothing—you miss nothing. You know—your life's on the line; your life's on the line; you're missing nothing. Every sense—every—all these new senses come and it's—and not that I'm—I—I don't do it for the thrill. I'm a complete chicken; I promise you I am . . . I do it for the money. And people say, 'Oh, you like it.' I don't like it; it's too much stress. But is there something nice about that feeling of being in the moment and suddenly you have accessed all these other senses? Yes. When you get the money home, it's, you know, you're just exhausted . . . It takes me about four days to come down.

CK directly likened the performance of armed robbery to that of professional show jumping. In his view, once the preparation had taken place and the event was about to begin, one enters a state of automaticity:

> Like, I feel pretty—you know, I'm pretty relaxed at that stage, pretty relaxed. Once the nerves are . . . It's like when you ride out to the judge to tip your hat in a jumping event. Like, your guts are going, you know; you're thinking, 'Oh, it's going to be a big event.' As soon as you tip the judge—tip your hat—and the judge rings the bell (*snap of fingers*), bang. Then you are just in the zone and off you go . . . It's automatic. It's the same with the show jumping—same—same—same. There's a lot of nerve. Show jumping is pretty elite too.

Many analyses of flow have indeed focused on competitive and often risky activities such as sports—motor racing, for instance, as illustrated by the Formula One driver Ayrton Senna, who famously described the trance-like state he entered during a race at the Monaco Grand Prix, quoted in Chapter 2 (see 'Affect as transcendence'). Key features of this 'optimal experience' outlined by Csikszentmihalyi are the distortion of time, in conjunction with a sense of omnipotence and automaticity. David (34) explains that 'everything goes really slow with extreme situations', enabling more to be achieved; like CK, he experiences a sense of precognition:

> That slow motion comes into play and it feels like you can do a lot more, and you do. Like, it's really—it's all happening; it's like autopilot and it's all happening. And you already know, like, what's coming a couple of minutes ahead and you're already, sort of like, your head's going like crazy and . . . you're ready for if something happens.

Daniel (28) was more instrumental in seeking to alter his affective state and reported that he would deliberately enter an 'unthinking' transcendental state in order to suppress any empathetic emotions towards the victim(s) that might inhibit the 'success' of the robbery:

> Okay, I didn't say this—I didn't tell you this. You know, when you do it [robbery], you're very nervous because now I'm going to do something extreme—even to me, it was so extreme. And so—so what I did was I blanked my brain out. I totally, like, blanked it out, you know; I wasn't thinking. Have you tried to, like, do the high ropes and stuff? That sort of thing or bungee jumping and stuff, you know? When you make the decision—you know, when—when you try to analyse it: 'No, no, no'—you know—'I'm not going to do it'—blah, blah, blah. But then you just say, 'Fuck it, just jump.' Yeah? That's exactly what happens. So then somehow—not just me, even my friend—we turn into somebody—*something* else. We don't think; just totally acting on our instincts. And I'm not proud of this, but we were quite—I mean, we were ingenious when we were calm—in that situation; we were extremely calm. We're not—our emotion was not fluctuating. We're totally out of sympathy with—we don't have sympathy towards—anybody at all. No sympathy. None.

For some in the present study, the extremity of behaviour that armed robbery requires triggered a subsumption of the self into an all-encompassing reality in which their senses became hyper-alert. Some of these offenders were consciously provoking their transcendence into a flow state through the use of all-encompassing extreme violence and risk.

Blowing the lid: violence as a relief valve

Tommy outlined how committing a robbery could serve in part as a relief valve for stress that built up in his life:

> Like, it did feel, like, pretty good, yeah, because so much stress built up and, after threatening someone with whatever sort of weapon and then feeling, like, a relief after that because you've let your anger and stress out—and it was a good rush and it started to become like an addictive rush.

Similarly, Max claimed that none of the aggravated robberies he'd committed was driven by the prospect of financial gain, but rather as a means to express the violence and anger that built up over days of heavy drug use: 'A lot of the robberies I've done, like, even that [supermarket robbery] in the shopping centre, like, I never needed the money; it was more of a—I don't know if it was a sort of thrill or just—I don't know.'

The smallest thing could be turned into a just provocation for Max. He was 23 years old and 2.5 years into a 6.5-year sentence for armed robbery with wounding. He'd first been in trouble with the police at the age of 16, for failing to move on and resisting arrest. Just one week later he committed his first street robbery, which he claimed was to avenge his ten-year-old nephew who had been 'bashed by some older blokes'. His first robbery of a commercial premises, armed with a screwdriver, followed shortly after. Max's crimes quickly escalated as his ice addition rocketed to 'half an eight ball a day' at a cost of $1,000.[1] The methamphetamine fuelled an intense revelry that would last for several days:

> I used to go out Wednesday night, and Thursday, Friday, Saturday … Sleep Sunday and Monday and [then] go out again. At the start it was fine, [but] come Friday and Saturday night, when I'd been awake for a while, I started to get aggressive and the fights started happening then, when I'd been up for a few days.

Describing a particularly violent street robbery of a young man in his twenties whom he and his friends had stopped to ask directions, Max explained

[1] An 'eight ball' is 1/8th of an ounce or 3.5 grams.

that financial gain was not a motivating, or even contributing, factor for him; he 'really didn't need the money':

> I think it was just out of anger really. Like, I pulled up [in the car] in Murralong—me and my friends. We drove around, and we dropped off my friend's girlfriend and we got lost on this country road and I was driving. I'd been up—up for a few days and I was, like—how do you say it—I'd get in the shits really, with me mates telling me, 'Go this way; go that way.' And I seen this bloke walking down the street, so I pulled up and told my mate in the passenger seat, 'Ask him for directions,' and I put my head back in the seat to have a little power nap. And I come to and the blokes kicked the side of the car and him and my friend were arguing, and I said, 'What's going on?' and he goes, 'He's being a smart arse.' I said, 'Get out of the car and flog him, or I will,' and my mate goes, laughing, goes, 'Oh, you do it then.' And, for some reason, there was a knife in the sun visor and I grabbed that, got out of the car, put the knife to his throat and said, 'What the fuck are you doing kicking my car?' and he laughed. He grabbed me by the shirt and he laughed at me. I said, 'Do you think I'm fucking joking with you?' and, um, he pushed me and I put the knife to his throat and, um, he pushed me and ran and it cut his neck and I chased him and—it was 175 metres and then he fell. He kicked out at me and I stabbed him twice in the leg and, um, grabbed his wallet off him and then, yeah, walked back to the car and we just ended—we ended up throwing his wallet out of the window down the road. Yeah. Yeah, he just—I guess he just caught me on the wrong day, huh!

I was interested in how indifferent Max seemed to be to the extremities of violence that he had used, and whether there was a rational calculation in his mind about how far he took it. He told me it was about taking control: 'I got to be in control. I ... have to go in there straight away and take control of the situation, and the best way to do that is with, like, aggression or violence.' I went on to ask him if it was a deliberate decision to stab the man in the leg in a bid to avoid a lethal wound. 'Yes,' he tells me.

> He was on his back and ... and I leaned forward and the way I was swinging, I was going for his neck. But suddenly, in a split second, instead of going like that [*indicates aiming at the neck*], I jumped back and got him in the upper thigh. I thought I missed because it went in so easy, so I done it again. And I got back in the car and my mate said, 'What

> happened?' and I said, 'I don't know,' and he turned on the interior light and I was covered in blood.

Some theories locate humiliation at the core of understanding violence and it is an established view in psychology that feelings of inferiority or low self-esteem predispose people to aggressive or violent behaviour. For example, the psychoanalytical theory of violence presented by Gilligan (1996) suggests that perpetrators use violence to attain a perceived measure of justice by punishing those who they feel have unjustly injured or humiliated them. This can be either direct aggression, targeting the individual who administered the threat to their ego, or displaced aggression, directed towards someone else, who was not responsible for the ego threat.

In their study of violent men in deindustrialized communities in the north of England, Ellis et al. (2017) suggest that early experiences of traumatic victimization encouraged the participants in their sample to grow into men of enviable violent capacity and significant cultural reputation. Such displaced aggression serves as a means of protecting oneself from social situations that generate embarrassment, or the threat of embarrassment. Walker and Bright (2009) claim that, due to their early experiences, individuals develop core beliefs about being vulnerable and weak; violence is an attempt to protect themselves against further injury (humiliation) and the perceived lowering of self-worth and pride. Any sense of impending humiliation activates these negative core beliefs, making the individual believe that someone has made them look foolish and that this perpetrator is deserving of punishment (see Lambe et al., 2018). In line with these theories, the humiliations of being lost and the victim kicking his car triggers a violent haze in Max. He feels compelled to respond and, given the fact that he had been on an intense drug binge, his violence is particularly vicious.

Revenge and resentment

Not all motivating emotions are experientially positive. Some described revenge, shame, and guilt as part of the reason for their offences. Jez was a married, hard-working civil engineer in his twenties when his difficulties began. He had been taking cocaine recreationally for several years and began 'a bit of dealing on the side'. Now aged 49, he tells me that it was falling victim to a scam that bred resentment and an overwhelming desire to regain the money that he had lost through the con.

> I became overly addicted—addicted to, um, the cocaine and also the lifestyle I was living. Um, it got to a point where I invested some money in a company with my cousin who is now deceased. Um, when the internet first came out to Australia, it was in the nineties and we each put in, as shareholders, an X-amount of money, um, but we found out that we got robbed. We didn't know. I didn't know; my cousin surely didn't know. So we lost, you know, a certain amount of money because it was the first franchise on the internet that came to Australia. So, unbeknownst to me, we've lost all that money. But a mitigating circumstance of why I went out and committed what I done is that, firstly, I lost the money through the [major] bank. So I took resentment towards them for not paying back the money. And somebody just said to me, 'Well, go and rob the bank.' So I did. I took matters into my own hands and kept going and going and going till I got caught.

Jez told me that he had committed 12 armed robberies throughout his criminal career and assured me that he had been convicted of all of them.

Maru had been in and out of juvie since the age of 14. He had run away from home at 13 and quickly became involved in selling drugs. He had gone to live with his cousin in Sydney who he tells me was well known—and liked—and in the early 2000s was making a lot of money dealing drugs in the notorious Kings Cross area.[2] To Maru as a young teenager, his older cousin's lifestyle and the respect that it brought him offered an attractive existence and he eagerly wanted to follow in his footsteps.

MARU: I used to look up to one of my cousins and I just wanted to be like him all the time, you know? We never had money when I was growing up, so I'd see some of my family making money and stuff and I wanted to be like them. My cousin—he was cool because everyone used to talk about

[2] Colloquially known as 'the Cross', the Kings Cross area of Sydney, with a high density of nightclubs, late night bars, brothels, and strip clubs, was notorious for organized crime in the 1990s and 2000s. Since controversial 'lockout laws' (licensing law reforms), introduced with the objective of reducing alcohol-fuelled violence, were enacted in 2014, several nightclubs and pubs in the area have closed down and there has been a corresponding significant reduction in non-domestic assault incidents in the area (Donnelly and Poynton, 2019).

him. Like, everyone liked him and that. He was into selling drugs and he was a very good fighter. We all grew up around boxing and he was, like, *the one*. He was better than most of us.

ET: Where is your cousin now?

MARU: He's dead. I saw it. He got shot. He was into robbing and shooting in the Cross and he upset the bloke that was in charge.

After the altercation in which Maru witnessed his cousin being killed, he explains that he tried to establish his own patch in another suburb, but it was not successful. He joined a gang in search of the 'camaraderie' he felt he had lost with the death of his cousin and 'started doing anything to make money', including armed robberies. The sadness and seething anger that Maru felt about the loss of his cousin never left him. He was eager to avenge his murder, setting in motion a violent retaliatory spiral that would result in him being shot on two separate occasions, as well as his repeated incarceration.

> I got the guy that killed my cousin. I shot him in the legs and, um, that was the whole drama, you know. Like, there was a bloke that was very, very up there, you know? I thought he was cool with me, you know. But, when I shot the guy who shot my cousin, I found out that, you know, they're really close. So then he come back on me and . . . I was shot twice. I thought the only way I could sort it out is if I come to jail and fix it up from jail, you know. It was stupid thinking. I was just in a panic, you know, and worried about the guy telling the police about me shooting him. And I was worried about other stuff too: about my house, my work, and my family. So I thought the only way I could fix it is to come to jail. When I got to jail, I sorted it out from jail, you know. He had boys in jail and he had some things that he wanted me to do for him in jail, you know? So I got in contact with him and he told me, like, I had to do a couple of things. There was a couple of people that—that had to be shut up that were going Crown witness against him. So—yeah. Just that whole chapter is just a totally different story, you know, but definitely I sorted it. It's been a mess. But I, I think I sorted it out well and, to me, I think that coming into jail was worth it for me, you know, the—for those armed robberies, you know. To me, I think I done the right thing. It cost me three and a half years, four years, but, you know, just everything got sorted. It took ages, but I sorted it out.

Shame and guilt

Some of the participants experienced intense feelings of guilt and shame following their crimes, particularly if somebody had been hurt. Tommy (24) admitted that he vomited after several of the armed robberies he had committed.

> I wasn't concerned about the money. I'm driving away and I've got the car door open and I'm driving like 80ks down a 50-kilometre street to get away and I'm spewing out the door. I didn't care how much money I had. I thought, 'Far out, this bloke's dying'—do you know what I mean? 'He's in there; he's had a heart attack', and—and I'm dead set throwing up out the door because I'm thinking, 'No!' I nearly crashed the car. Hit another car; took the mirror off the car. Driving; just, me head's all over the place. I pull over in this reserve near the creek. I jump out, spew everywhere. And I sat at the creek and didn't even look at the money bag for two, three hours. I just sat at the creek, stressing, like, 'Oh, no, no'—you know—and I'm crying and everything, you know. I honestly thought he was having a heart attack. I thought he was—like, something was really wrong with him, you know, and I felt bad. I—I—I—I felt, 'No; look, I'm—I'm gone,' you know, like, and—and that's why, as I said, like, I took a lot more time than I should have. And I was trying to be—I was being nice to him. You know, I said, you know, like, 'Just give me the money, mate; look, where is it?' and, 'Oh, look, I'm so sorry; look'—you know—'are you all right? Sit down; mate, sit down.' And he just pointed to the drawer and I said, 'Yeah, thank you, mate,' and, 'Just stay there'—right—'sit down,' and I took the money and left, you know, but—

Tommy attributed his physical reaction in part to the surge of adrenaline coursing through his body, but also acknowledged that he was most likely to have such a severe physical response when he knew he had really scared somebody. He went on to explain that the image of his victims would often appear to him in flashbacks in prison.

> [W]hen I'm holding 'em and I'm looking in their eyes, I'm trying to be serious, and—and I know I have to be serious because this is what I do, this is what I have to do; but then the—the kind heart comes out and—and I—I feel bad, you know. And I try and talk to 'em and they're freaking out and, you know—and heaps of 'em are, like, dropped, collapsed, shaking,

> like, just in fear, or I've thought with that person he was having a heart attack, and the look on their faces is—oh, look, I—I still, like, get flashbacks in me head now of people's faces and that and I—I—I cry in me cell. Me cellmate's like, 'Are you all right, mate?' and I'm like, 'Mate, look, I'm—I'm just not with it, hey; like, I can't'—and he goes, 'What's wrong?' and I'm—I—I try and explain to him, 'Look, this is what's happened'—you know—'while I'm'—you know—'since I've been in and this is what happened outside,' you know. And he goes, 'Well, look, these programs are really helping you because you wouldn't sit there crying, if you didn't have remorse for these people and you didn't want to change your life; and'—you know—'if you didn't care about 'em, you'd—you'd just be like, "Oh, stuff 'em; I'll get out; I—that's all right; I'll—I'll go back there and I'll kill 'em next time because they rang the coppers",' which is wrong. You know?
>
> **(Tommy, 24)**

Jack Katz (1999: 156) outlines how

> shame is not just a unique way of seeing oneself from the standpoint of encountered or imagined others; it is also distinguished by a sense of negative practical possibilities. The coherent behavioural practices that follow shame are metamorphoses of shame into some other emotionally charged conduct, such as crying or anger, which cover shame with their own expressive logics.

Some would use techniques of neutralization to brush aside feelings of guilt and shame (see Chapter 5), but for some, such as Tommy, these feelings would burst through in the form of flashbacks.

Conclusion

It is important to recognize that the elements that embody criminal behaviour—its emotions, its performativity, and its visceral qualities—can be consciously pursued for their generative potentials. Affective transgression expands the scope of criminological enquiry, inviting consideration of emotions, the body, and identity to help us to understand *why* it is that this crime is pursued over others. The analysis provided in this chapter responds to the need to connect the visceral with the cultural, the somata with the social.

PART FOUR
SUCH IS LIFE

9

Getting Caught and Doing Time

> How can a poor bloke in a flannelette shirt, from Mount Druitt, afford a brand new $70,000 car? That's going to attract some attention, isn't it?
>
> I don't know how they classify this as being rehabilitating, because it's not. It's a university for criminals to get more advanced. If you cage up a dog ... If you treat 'em like an animal, they're going to turn out like an animal; it's simple as that.
>
> **(Kimsan, 39)**

Given that the interviews all took place in prison, obviously all of the robbers had been convicted, of some of their crimes at least. The contexts in which they were caught ranged from being arrested at the scene to being detained months, even years, after the offence. Some individuals were convicted when an accomplice provided evidence about them in order to reduce their own sentence, and some claimed that it was wives or girlfriends who had reported them. Trust was in short supply. This chapter outlines the ways in which offenders were caught, their views on the process, and experiences of prison life.

Snitches and show-offs

'It gets to the stage where it's very hard to trust people,' Robert (51) explained, highlighting how betrayal could result in a retaliatory response:

> Yeah, I have been betrayed and—well, it's not a nice feeling—do you know what I mean? And—what it does: it puts you in that situation where

Armed Robbers. Emmeline Taylor, Oxford University Press. © Emmeline Taylor 2022.
DOI: 10.1093/oso/9780198855132.003.0009

> you feel you have to do something about it, you know. And, like, you know, sometimes you do things. You don't really want to do it; part of you doesn't want to do it, but part of you feels like you're obliged to do it. I know it sounds silly, but it's just honour, a bit of morals. It's a bit being hurt because someone's betrayed you. You know, it guts you when—and it's always someone you'd least expected. Usually the person you've worried about spewing his beans is the one who's rock solid. But it's—it's usually the person you least expected to who does the damage to you. Do you know what I mean? That's—that's my experience in life. Of course, you will get good friends who would—I won't say 'gladly do a life sentence for you,' but they'd do it because they'd feel like that's just how the cards fell; but they're very few and far between.

It wasn't always people deliberately snitching; sometimes an offender might brag about the crime or make large purchases that would arouse suspicion.

> You have very big issues with braggarts, or some people might not tell anyone about it, but their actions—they might as well scream it, yeah. Do you know what I mean? Like, you know, suddenly they've got a new car. You know, they never worked in their life and, you know, now they have got a $30,000 car.

Relatively hidden in our understanding of armed robbery is the role of women—girlfriends, wives, and mothers. In the present study it was not uncommon for the robbers to describe the women in their lives as part of the motivation for their crimes. In some instances this was through a desire to provide financial support for them (although at times this was likely to be a means of justifying their illegal behaviour), while in others, women were described as encouraging the robberies so that they could enjoy the spoils, as well as experience second-hand the danger and thrill that they presented. However, several of the men claimed that it was a significant female in their life who had 'dobbed' them in to the police.

The reasons for doing so were highly complex. Overall, and in contrast to being snitched on by a 'co-ie', the men were forgiving of women in their lives who had provided evidence against them. There were two main reasons for this. One was that they believed that it was a concern for their welfare, a deep-rooted benevolent maternalism, that drove women, particularly mothers, to turn in their men in order to protect them from the dangers of the criminal world. The other was recognition that their behaviour was potentially endangering the women in their life, and often their children, and so reporting to the police was motivated by self-preservation. CK tells me that it was his now ex-wife who had reported him to the police, but that he was empathetic of her reasons.

CK: Even though the sentence is massive, you know, I've got gorgeous kids and they love me. Even my ex-wife who told on me, I'm not even dirty on her. She went to the police and told 'em about our lives—about our whole lives, yeah.

ET: Why did she tell on you after all that time?

CK: Oh, you know. I had a gorgeous girlfriend. We—we—there—there—there was a blow-up over it, you know—domestic type stuff; domestic stuff. She knew that once she moved, she really—she did it to get rid of me really. So, when she hit me, she knew she had to hit me hard. She knew she—she tried to get me life.

ET: Did she not implicate herself?

CK: Yeah, she did; she got immunity from prosecution, yeah, to give her a 128 certificate.[1] She got immunity from prosecution; yeah, she did, she did. She told it—and all these ones that I'm not talking to you about: they know about 'em. She told 'em about 'em all, but she—they didn't have any evidence. No; no evidence and no evidence anywhere—anywhere. The work was proper.

Anthony (38), incarcerated at Beach Head Prison, told me that his girlfriend would enjoy the excitement of the robberies that he committed and would often be present, usually waiting in the car. She eventually provided evidence against him, which he was pragmatic about:

> She, um, went crown witness against me—so she got immunity. But I—like, I wasn't going to—I don't know; yeah. I told her to do whatever she had to do to get out of it, you know. I would never want a girl to go to jail.

Maru (30) and his robbery group had established punishments for anyone who was found to have jeopardized the anonymity of their crimes:

[1] Section 128 of the Evidence Act 1995 (Commonwealth) deals with the privilege against self-incrimination. A certificate is commonly sought to protect a client from criminal charges.

> There was a couple of times a couple of boys, um, said stuff to girls they didn't even know; they'd just start bragging with them and stuff like that about where they'd get the money and ... Oh, they'd cop it; they used to cop it ... We used to make 'em walk the line. We'd all, like—like, we used to line up on each side and make 'em walk to the end; they'd just get beat up in the middle.

Maru went on to say that it was just a few bruises that would be inflicted by the 12-strong group, six on each side, who would set upon the loose-lipped accomplice. Only once did Maru say that an accomplice was beaten unconscious in this procedure and that was because he had bought a car using cash from the robbery, despite living only on social security benefits.

Carceral topography in the land of plenty: prisons profile in Australia

As of June 2020, corrective services operated 115 custodial facilities across Australia, comprising 88 government-operated prisons, ten privately operated prisons, four transitional centres, and thirteen 24-hour court cell complexes. It has been estimated that Australian prisons are the fifth most expensive among 29 countries in the Organisation for Economic Co-operation and Development (OECD) (Bushnell, 2017); nationally, expenditure (net of revenues) on corrective services was $3.64 billion for prisons and $0.71 billion for community corrections in 2018–19 (Productivity Commission, 2020).[2]

The prison population has overall been increasing in Australia, doubling over the last two decades from 21,714 adult prisoners in 2000 to 43,028 in June 2019, the most recent annual figures available before the onset of the Covid 19 pandemic (Australian Bureau of Statistics, 2019).[3] The flow of

[2] The top five countries by annual amount spent per prisoner were claimed to be: Sweden ($193,311), Norway ($190,035), the Netherlands ($149,079), Luxembourg ($112,776), and Australia ($109,821). The OECD average was estimated to be $69,319 (Bushnell, 2017).

[3] The Australian Bureau of Statistics (ABS) provides an annual overview of prison statistics, aligning with the Australian financial year (1 July–30 June). The statistics, published at abs.gov.au, are derived from information collected by the ABS from corrective services agencies in each state and territory. Details are provided on the number of people in correctional institutions, including the type of prisoner (sentenced prisoners, unsentenced prisoners (remandees), and post-sentence prisoners), imprisonment rates, most serious offence/charge, and sentence length. Information is also presented on prisoner characteristics, including age, sex, nationality, and Indigenous status.

prisoners into prison per year is always far more than the 'snapshot' population in the annual June census, due to the high numbers of remand and short-sentence prisoners. As is the case in all countries, males make up the vast majority of the Australian prisoner population (39,538 prisoners; 92 per cent of total prisoners). Interestingly, prisoners with an offence/charge of robbery had the lowest median age (30 years) of all offence categories.

The growing proportion of unsentenced prisoners is of particular concern. It has been increasing since 2010; 33 per cent (14,210 prisoners) of the prison population in June 2019 had not yet been tried. The median time on remand for prisoners was 3.1 months. This appeared to be a relatively short wait compared to some of the inmates I interviewed. For example, Dave (36) who I interviewed at Privatefield Prison in November 2016 was expecting his trial for attempted robbery to commence in January 2017, at which point, he said, it would have been two years since being remanded in custody. While he was frustrated by the slowness of the process, he told me it wasn't unusual, 'Well, there's others been on remand for three years, four years or something, you know.' This means that a sizeable number of individuals might serve longer in prison than the sentence that they eventually receive; some indeed might not receive a custodial sentence at all, or have it suspended.

Private prisons

Walking along a path that flanked an external brick wall to Privatefield Prison, I heard a 'wolf whistle' from above. Looking up, I could see several men leaning out of their cells, eyeing me suspiciously and gesturing obscenities as I passed. I could smell wafts of chemicals like burnt plastic on the air; surely they weren't smoking ice? I quickened my pace and eventually reached a turnstile that I couldn't pass through. Looking around, I could not see any prison officers. I stood waiting for someone to appear to let me through, or at least validate my presence, but there was nobody in sight. After a few minutes the metal barrier made an audible click and I could now push my way through—somebody somewhere must have been watching my progress through the prison.

Eventually I found the segregation wing that I had been looking for. An inmate carrying a broom rushed towards me: 'Are you a solicitor? Are you a solicitor? I need a solicitor. I need help. Can you help me? I need someone to help me.' He was almost hysterical, looking searchingly into my eyes, his pupils were dilated despite the bright sun, and he was struggling to focus. Sweating profusely in the humid heat, he had clearly taken some substances, legal or otherwise. 'I'm sorry, I'm not a legal professional. Is there an officer here that can help you?' He stared at me, slowly processing the words I was saying, before turning and running away across the grass that separated the wings, waving the broom aloft with both hands. Things felt edgy.

I found a prison officer, explained who I was and who I was scheduled to interview. I was put in a small office with a large Perspex window. 'Is there a duress button in here?' I enquired. Many interview rooms have a panic alarm, usually under the desk so that you can discreetly alert officers if an inmate is becoming threatening or violent. 'No, not in here,' the officer replied, with a somewhat nervous laugh. The interviewee, Dave, was brought in. His wrists were cuffed together at the front and, as he sat down, he deliberately banged the chain shackling him loudly on the table. Dave has several tattoos that have become blue and blurred as the ink has blown out. A spider's web rises up from his t-shirt and wraps around his neck symbolizing a long prison sentence—a life spent snared in the tangled traps of the criminal justice system.

I start by thanking him for returning the reply slip and agreeing to the interview. 'I don't know what you're on about,' he tells me, noticeably slurring his words. Due to the long process of negotiating access, over three months had passed since my letters had been distributed, so I tried to jog his memory.

ET: I'm from a university. Do you recall me writing to you a few months ago?
DAVE: Nope.
ET: I sent you a letter that looked like this?
DAVE: Nope.
ET: It had a green slip in it and a pre-paid envelope?
DAVE: Nope.
ET: Okay, no problem, let me tell you who I am and why I'm here.

I outlined the project and ran through the information sheet and consent form. Dave looked confused. 'I've never done an armed robbery. That's for silly cunts. I'm in here for rape and attempted murder.' Dave went on to tell me how he enjoys smashing women's heads against walls—women who look just like me apparently. He was now in the 'boneyard' (segregation unit) after stabbing his cellmate with a shiv. Asking him what his MIN was, I realized that the wrong Dave had been brought to the room. I felt an imminent sense of danger as Dave looked at me with a menacing expression intended to intimidate. I could not think straight and did not know whether to scream or stay quiet, to plead or exude a fierceness of my own—in many ways probably similar dilemmas to those racing through the head of someone cornered by an unpredictable armed robber.

I know from my training as a researcher that it is important to navigate your way out of these situations carefully so as not to make matters worse. I explained to Dave that there had been a mix-up. Apologizing for the confusion, I slowly rose from my chair and told him that I'd speak to one of the officers. Keeping my eyes on him, I reached to grasp the door handle, but to my alarm there was nothing there. Rather, where it should have been, I find an empty circular hole stuffed with a paper towel. I was locked in. But, worse than that, there was no one around. I started by knocking on the door and calling out. Nothing. I banged on the Perspex window, trying to look confident and remain calm. 'Locked in, are we?' Dave asked wryly. 'No, no, they'll be here in a sec.' After what felt like an eternity, an officer appeared and let me out. I was furious.

After Dave had been escorted away, I asked the officer why the door handle was missing. Somewhat nonchalantly, he explained that they were so understaffed that the only way to 'manage' visits to the boneyard by legal professionals, counsellors, psychologists, and researchers was to lock them in the room so the inmate could not attempt to escape while the officers were dealing with other matters. I was astounded that the door handle had been deliberately removed by the prison staff. This was a very high-risk strategy. The officer went on to tell me that it was the least of their worries—there were simply no staff and they could not be in two places at once. As a result, they had devised their own methods to attempt to contain prisoners when the usual protocols were unfeasible.

I was very sympathetic to the situation that the officers found themselves in at Privatefield Prison—these were high-risk, violent, and volatile inmates—and they were not being given the resources to manage them safely by the company, GEO Group Australia, which had held the contract to run the prison since 2009. Between 2016 and September 2018, there were 11 deaths in custody, seven of which were suicides:

> Of the 11 deaths in custody, seven were by suicide, one patient died of endocarditis, one patient died of sepsis, one death occurred while the patient was undergoing detoxification, and one death occurred as a result of a cerebral aneurysm. There were six serious incidents. Three were

> due to self harm that required hospitalisation and surgical intervention; two were due to self harm that required hospitalisation; and one was due to an assault that required hospitalisation and surgical intervention.
> **(NSW Legislative Council, 2018: 18)**

I was not surprised when, not long after my visit, the prison suffered a number of serious incidents. In early 2016, 40 inmates attacked prison guards, who had to barricade themselves inside a safe room until special operations forces arrived and seized back control. Later that year, in December 2016, an inmate stole a set of keys as they were released from custody, resulting in numerous locks having to be replaced. Following that, and finally triggering the Corrective Services NSW commissioner to launch an unprecedented intervention at the facility, a video taken inside a cell on a contraband smartphone went viral on YouTube in 2017. In the video, the inmate flaunted homemade weapons, including a 'slasher' and drugs, which he claimed was ice. He added a voiceover:

> On a day-to-day basis this place is a dead-set joke. Right now in my cell I have got a mobile phone. Why have I got a mobile phone? It's because screws bring mobile phones into the jail for money. Alright now, why am I carrying around a knife like that? [*shows blade to camera*] . . . Okay, why have I got a slasher? Why do I need to slash people? Do I need to show you the slash marks [*indicates damage on the cell wall*]? That's just an example of what it can do to your throat. Now you see all that [*shows small plastic bag of white powder*], that's the drug ice, why have I got it? Huh . . . because I can . . . Let's get to the point of this jail. Now this jail is ruining lives. It is killing the young people, [it] is dead-set terrorizing.[4]

Not long afterwards, it was confirmed that the contract with GEO Group Australia was not going to be renewed at the end of its term. An inquiry was launched that found, among other things, that GEO's staffing of the prison, unsafe work practices, and lack of management action enabled 'an occupationally dangerous culture to flourish' (NSW Legislative Council, 2018: 19). However, rather than returning the prison to state management, the $1.3 billion

[4] The video has since been removed from YouTube, but not before it was picked up and distributed by major media outlets, including the ABC and The Mirror newspaper. See https://www.mirror.co.uk/news/uk-news/convict-films-himself-inside-prison-10773254 (accessed 10 November 2021).

contract was awarded to a joint venture between the US prisons contractor, Management & Training Corporation (MTC) and Australian-based provider Broadspectrum, commencing in April 2019. One former Australian prison superintendent described the decision as 'incomprehensible', given MTC's 'atrocious track record in the USA' (cited in Begley, 2019: n.p.). Only time will tell whether the new contract and recommendations from the inquiry into the failures at the prison will improve conditions for staff and inmates. At the time of writing, the Public Service Association (PSA) had already reported that Privatefield correctional officers had suffered a record number of assaults within the first six months of MTC–Broadspectrum control (Begley, 2019).

'The private sector can do it cheaper and better,' the 1988 *Kennedy Report* confidently claimed, even before any privatization[5] of the prison estate had occurred in Australia (Kennedy, 1988: 88). In the intervening years, the private prison estate has grown to the extent that Australia currently has a higher proportion of its prisoners in private prisons than any other country in the world (Sands et al., 2019).[6] In 2019, almost one in five prisoners (18.8 per cent of the prison population) was held in privately operated facilities. In the state of Victoria, almost a third (31 per cent) of prisoners are held in private prisons—the highest proportion in the country, and the highest of any jurisdiction in the world (Sands et al., 2019).

Overall, private contractors operate ten facilities in five different states: New South Wales, Queensland,[7] South Australia, Victoria, and

[5] 'Privatization' of prisons often refers not to private ownership and control of an enterprise, but rather to contract management, whereby a private-sector company (or non-government organization) manages institutions that remain a public-sector responsibility. There are different gradations of privatizing, ranging from contracting out particular services, such as the supply of meals or laundry, to the private-sector design, construction, and financing of a new facility, which is then leased back to the state (Harding, 1992).

[6] The US Department of Justice under the Obama administration announced a commitment to reduce, and ultimately seek to end, its use of privately operated prisons. Several plans to build new facilities such as a 1,000-bed immigration detention centre in Texas were cancelled. On the day of the announcement, the stock of the GEO Group, one of the USA's largest private prison operators, fell from $21.53 to $13.01 a share, as investors clearly realized the impact of the decree. In 2015, 45 per cent of the company's revenue came from government agencies. In the weeks running up to the 2016 presidential election, GEO Corrections Holdings Inc., a GEO Group subsidiary, donated hundreds of thousands of dollars to the pro-Trump political action committee (PAC). Furthermore, US private prison companies routinely lobby Congress for lengthier prison sentences; their vested interest is clear. As the media do, powerful companies can shape public sentiment and drive an agenda of more punitive sanctions.

[7] It was announced in March 2019 that Queensland will transfer both of its privately operated prisons, the Arthur Gorrie Correctional Centre and Southern Queensland Correctional Centre, from private to public control. The decision came after the completion of the *Taskforce Flaxton Report* (Crime and Corruption Commission, 2018), which highlighted significant levels of corruption.

Western Australia. Although many are contracted to companies that are Australian-sounding, such as GEO Group Australia Pty Ltd, they are typically subsidiaries of US-owned globally operating huge security companies: GEO Group Inc., G4S, and Serco. Not only does this mean that any profits these companies generate are lost to Australia, but—perhaps more importantly—cultural specificities become diluted or altogether ignored. Does Australia really want to emulate the style and culture of the criminal justice system in the USA, a country that incarcerates more people per capita than any other nation (currently 655 per 100,000, according to the World Prison Brief (2019))?

Prisoner experience

David Biles (2012) claims private prisons are 'more popular' with prisoners, but Dave (36), at Privatefield Prison, didn't agree. He'd been in 'segro' (segration) for two weeks after throwing hot water at another inmate and had been informed that he was to expect to stay there for three months. As I sat and talked with him, he became increasingly preoccupied with a very sore-looking rash on his inner forearm; the skin was red raw and blistered in places. I presumed it was bed bugs and made a mental note to wash my clothes on the hottest cycle when I got home. I asked him about how he felt being in segregation for a prolonged period of time and found out much more about the operation of the private prison than I was expecting.

ET: How do you find it in segro?

DAVE: Ah, I just wanted to have a rest, you know, because I was out there and—and I been using drugs and that and all me arm's all—all infected and—and sore.

ET: It looks very painful. Were you using drugs in prison?

DAVE: Yeah, in the prison.

ET: What drugs are you using?

DAVE: Heroin. That was a couple of weeks ago and all me arm's all infected and—and, um, I think I've got an infection in the arm or something.

ET: So it is pretty easy to get drugs in the prison?

DAVE: Yeah, it's simple; yeah, easy.

ET: Is that something that the prison officers know about?

DAVE: Ah, I don't—I don't think they really care, you know, what's going on, you know, so, it could be them—I'm not sure how it gets in, but basically, it's there, you know; so, if you want it, it's there, yeah.

ET: This is a private prison, isn't it?

DAVE: Private, yeah.

ET: Is it different from when you were in Cessnock?

DAVE: Yeah. Well, um, that's Corrective Services; this is—this is private, you know, so—I prefer Corrective Services.

ET: Why's that?

DAVE: Well, um, in here it's much more easy, isn't it? And, um, in Cessnock it's actually done properly, you know. But here, just—everybody gets away with everything here, you know. Everything—everything—everybody gets away with everything. Some are just not running the same, you know. As I said all me arm is—I caught an infection, I think, in me arm, so—

ET: Do you get programmes here? Like to help with drugs?

DAVE: We get nothing here. They've stopped all the programmes, especially, um, for 'smack' inmates, you know.

There weren't bed bugs at Privatefield; it was infested with drugs. It became clear that Dave had been injecting heroin on the main wing and his arm had become severely infected with what looked like a staph infection commonly associated with intravenous drug use. I wondered if the deaths relating to endocarditis and sepsis could also be a result of injecting drugs in the prison.

Carceral capital: Australia's prison-industrial complex

In a large warehouse at Rural Prison, men were sweating over the construction of large cellular structures. 'What are you building?' I asked enthusiastically. 'Prison cells,' came the reply. I was taken aback. The men were constructing the very walls that would eventually confine them, and no doubt some of their sons, nephews, cousins. Digging one's own grave indeed. 'Are you not tempted to hide a chisel in the wall?' I joked, attempting to mask my unease. Another set of prisoners was packing small, zipped pouches. Upon closer inspection, I could see what they were: the business-class amenity packs for Qantas Airlines. The irony of incarcerated men, limited in their mobility, many shackled by structural disadvantage and poverty, stuffing luxury socks, eye masks, headphones into designer pouches for mobile elite customers traversing the world was certainly not lost on me.

At Rural Prison I was intrigued to see how the Correctional Services Industry (CSI) operated in practice. Inmates were employed in a variety of jobs, including engineering, manufacturing, and commercial laundry. On average 81 per cent of Australian adult prisoners are engaged in some form of employment (Productivity Commission, 2019), with some jobs contributing towards the operation and maintenance of the prison itself (including working in the kitchen, laundry, and grounds) and others fulfilling profit-making external contracts for private companies. For example, prisoners fulfilling contracts through CSI sew Australian flags and hospital bed linen, and Indigenous prisoners produce a range of artefacts and craft items for sale at a profit (Brook, 2017). It is noteworthy that the state of Victoria, with the highest proportion of inmates in privately operated prisons (31 per cent) also has the highest employment rate: 92 per cent of eligible prisoners are in employment (Brook, 2017).

Access to a captive labour force exempt from the minimum wage and not eligible for sick pay or annual leave is an enticing proposition for companies seeking to maximize profit. This was all too obvious for some participants who had experienced incarcerated labour:

> I'm working in the kitchen. Now, it's seven days a week—it keeps your mind occupied, but seven days a week and I get, what, 70 bucks? All right. But that's double shifts. So that's morning and afternoon; okay? So, think about this: why would companies come from America to Australia to lease—they don't buy the jail; they lease the jail. Now, if they're not making a profit, I don't know what else a company CEO would be doing here.
>
> **(Kimsan, 39)**

The 'prison-industrial complex' (PIC)[8] is a term used to describe a set of interrelated processes that inflates incarceration rates due to the profitability that prisons provide to the private companies that operate them, as

[8] Mike Davis is credited with coining the term 'prison-industrial complex', basing it on the former US president Dwight D. Eisenhower's use of the description the 'military-industrial complex' to convey the convergence of the state's military and private weapons industry (Sudbury, 2004). In his article, 'Hell factories in the field: a prison-industrial complex', Davis (1995), writing about the bloated Californian penal system, forewarns that 'its uncontrollable

well as to multiple companies that provide peripheral goods and services to the prison system (catering, uniforms, technological surveillance, and so on). According to Schlosser (1998: 54), the PIC is a set of bureaucratic, political, and economic interests that encourage increased spending on imprisonment, regardless of the actual need.

Under the PIC, the prison system succumbs to market imperatives to increase revenue. For example, it is argued that senior stakeholders undertake considerable lobbying of government to ensure that conditions favourable to a steady influx of prisoners, such as harsher sentencing, are maintained.

The commercial arm of Corrective Services NSW (CSI NSW) operates more than a hundred commercial business units and service industry teams in both metro and regional correctional centres across NSW. In 2016, CSI had an annual revenue of $113 million generating a $45.6 million profit (Brook, 2017). CSI NSW (2019) asserts that the arrangement is a win-win for industry and inmates:

> Industry benefits from access to an increasing range of manufacturing and other service capabilities provided by inmates, and inmates benefit by gaining work skills that enhance employment opportunities on release and successful reintegration into the community.

Scott (34) worked at the high-security prison he'd been moved to after a bungled escape at his previous jail. Monday to Friday he leaves his cell at 6:30 a.m. and goes to sit in front of a sewing machine where he makes workwear for the private sector. In return, he earns $40.60 a week that goes into his 'buy up' account to be spent on 'toiletries, food and stuff like that'. It has been argued that the relatively low cost of 'unfree labour' makes it difficult for the private sector to employ civilians and compete with prison labourers. For example, it is estimated that inmates earn a maximum of $70.55 for 30 hours of work a week, whereas an individual on the minimum wage would earn $719.20 a week, more than ten times as much (Wilkie, 2018).[9]

growth ought to rattle a national consciousness now complacent at the thought of a permanent prison class'.

[9] The NSW Government (2018: 2) denies that it operates with an unfair advantage to the private sector: 'CSI operates to strict ethical principles and is sensitive to potential impacts on businesses in the community. Potential exists for unfair advantage over businesses operating in the same sectors. For this reason, CSI is required to adhere to *Costing and Pricing Policies* which prescribe the methods by which all CSI commercial transactions are conducted to ensure that it is competing fairly with the private sector.'

It is a remarkable sleight of hand of post-industrialist capitalism: at the same time as many workers, particularly in regional areas of Australia, struggle to find paid employment in the manufacturing and industrial sector, contracts are being awarded to private-prison operators, almost exclusively from the USA, that outsource prison labour at a fraction of the cost. Some argue that capitalizing on the 'unfree labour' provided by a burgeoning prison population is essentially a form of modern slavery. In fact, in the USA in 2017, a class-action lawsuit was served on the GEO Group. It was alleged that they had violated anti-slavery laws by forcing approximately 60,000 current and former immigrants detained by Immigration and Customs Enforcement (ICE) to work for less than a dollar a day at its detention centre in Colorado (Philips, 2017).

There has been a radical shift in the labour market since Paul Willis published *Learning to Labour* (1977), calling forth new lessons beyond the correspondence between education and the workplace for many working-class men. The school production line identified by Willis has become fractured and is no longer routed only to the industrial workplace. Rather, prisons have become the relief valve, filtering off the already marginalized poor into carceral warehouses. Post-industrialism has brought with it

> the need for the management and control of a population that has become economically superfluous—particularly in urban deindustrialized zones ... Urban public schools have become increasingly connected ... to the criminal justice system and to the production of mass incarceration.
>
> **(Nolan and Anyon, 2004: 133–4)**

Writing about mass incarceration in the USA, Nolan and Anyon (2004) have argued that, far from 'learning to labour', working-class men, particularly men of colour, are 'learning to do time'. Not dissimilar processes appear to be taking place in Australia, with the pronounced over-representation of Indigenous Australians in prisons. As of June 2019, Aboriginal and Torres Strait Islanders make up just 3 per cent of the total Australian population, but account for over a quarter (28 per cent) of the total Australian prisoner population (Australian Bureau of Statistics, 2019). Concerningly, Indigenous Australians are the most incarcerated by percentage of their population (2,346 per 100,000) in the world.[10] It would seem that the free market ultimately seeks to profit from unfree labour.

[10] This statement was 'fact checked' by *The Conversation* after it was claimed on an episode of *Q&A* broadcast on 29 May 2017. Using data from the US Bureau of Justice Statistics and

Conclusion

Australia's prison system is characterized by a number of notable statistics: it incarcerates the highest proportion of prisoners in private prisons, it is the fifth most expensive prison system of OECD countries, and it also holds the shameful record of incarcerating the highest percentage of any ethnic group in the world. Privatization has been proposed as a way of providing prison services at a lower cost, with better efficiency, and stronger accountability. Yet in reality, the investigations that have been conducted in NSW and Queensland have shown that private prisons can quickly lead to dangerous environments for both prisoners and employees.

Notwithstanding the operational issues that have beset the privatization of prisons in Australia, there are much broader philosophical questions regarding the appropriateness of private entities enforcing the social contract that citizens hold with the state. In addition to the ethical dubiety of profiting from the misery of others, there are huge cultural differences in criminal justice policy and punishment that are overlooked when global for-profit conglomerates take over the prison estate.

the ABS, it found that Indigenous Australians are the most incarcerated by percentage of their population (2,346 per 100,000), followed by African-American people in the USA (2,207 per 100,000) (see The Conversation, 2017).

10
Such Is Life
Affect, Fatalism, and Crime

> In the end the money's not worth much; it goes through your fingers like sand.
>
> **(CK)**

The life trajectories of the armed robbers who participated in this study were by no means uniform, but stories of violent upbringings, abuse, neglect, homelessness, drug addiction, and feelings of low self-worth became familiar narratives. Their stories reveal the plurality of criminal subjects and the complex reasons why they engage in violent crime. Socialization and exposure to crime and violence from a young age can influence the likelihood of engaging in crime in later life. This was, moreover, exacerbated by multiple and varied factors such as parental neglect, harsh and inconsistent discipline, drug abuse, living in high-crime-rate areas, and experiencing a high level of socioeconomic disadvantage. Poor or non-existent school attendance, followed by the dissatisfaction of low-paid and precarious employment, or extended periods of unemployment, typified the lives of many of the offenders interviewed for this study. Everyday life was experienced as monotonous and dull, punctuated only by the highs of illicit drug taking or numbed by excessive alcohol use. Devoid of sensory stimulation, many would recklessly engage in criminal activities. It was clear that low self-esteem, a lack of prospects, and a quest to construct identity and meaning from meagre resources prompted the 'do or die' mentality deeply entrenched in Australian narratives of white masculinity. Extreme behaviour could resuscitate, as if through defibrillation, a life otherwise devoid of responsivity due to excessive drug use, depression, and lack of prospect, even if only temporarily.

Armed Robbers. Emmeline Taylor, Oxford University Press. © Emmeline Taylor 2022.
DOI: 10.1093/oso/9780198855132.003.0010

'Such is life' is still widely claimed to be Ned Kelly's final words. Irrespective of suggestions that this is somewhat unlikely (see Chapter 5), the phrase has taken on cultural meaning in the Australian psyche, symbolizing the plight of the underdog and a revered anti-authoritarian spirit. It captures a distinctive aspect of Australian masculinity, one based on blind courage, autonomy, and a certain degree of resignation and fatalism, the criminal manifestations of which have furnished the pages of this book. The national mythscapes curated in the post-war era to reimagine a shared identity and collective culture hold within them an instructive masculinity that, when applied to post-industrial communities, can easily be diverted into illicit activities. When subverted, the Australian Dream narrative becomes a Faustian exchange whereby men, lacking any other real prospects, roll the dice for the opportunity to experience hedonistic highs and total abandon in exchange for their liberty at the end of it all. Will (41) explained that armed robbers were 'stand-up kind of blokes' who had been jailed for 'having a go'. For many, even once incarcerated, the currency of armed robbery allows them to elevate their status above what they could ever achieve in the free world and a sense of camaraderie and mateship is secured among the other inmates.

The repression of emotion and affect in criminological theory

Many an undergraduate criminology student will attest that Cesare Lombroso's anthropometric studies and resulting thesis of degenerate heredity are ritually slayed in their introductory classes to criminology. Not surprisingly, the idea that the majority of criminals are 'born with' innate congenital defects that *cause* them to commit crime has been, for the vast majority of offenders, thoroughly debunked. Yet, although the implausibility of Lombroso's conception that atavists were evolutionary duds from a more primitive time is widely acknowledged, its dismissal has inflicted unfortunate and collateral damage. Any suggestion that physiological, visceral, and instinctive factors could coalesce with social structures or circumstances has been viewed suspiciously by criminologists. Writing about emotions, Hepburn (2003: 170) comments that we often 'think of them as linked in to physiology and sometimes, as things that burst through cultural restrictions as a legacy of a more primitive animal past'. The enduring distrust of, or even outright hostility towards, biological determinism has for a long time tarnished engagement with factors other than background social structures as precursors to criminal behaviour. More broadly, a 'fragile and shaky' relationship between biology and the social sciences has endured (Wetherell, 2012: 10). The outcome is that 'many established modes of criminological thought proceed in ways that ignore entirely, or at best gesture towards, the impact of emotions on their subject matter' (van Gelder et al., 2014: 1).

Hence, while the 'affective turn' has gained ground in social and cultural theory, it has struggled to find traction within criminology to the same extent as other cognate disciplines. Although Massumi (2015: 21) claims affect as 'a dimension of *every* event' (emphasis added), it has often been excluded from sociological enquiries of deviance, because the visceral components of social action are 'subjective and so beyond *direct* empirical measurement' (Jacques and Wright, 2010: 27). In a discipline that strives for objectivity and an observable reality, feelings and emotions are thought to be 'at best, unobservable or, at worst nothing real at all' (Jacques and Wright, 2010: 27). Van Gelder et al. (2014: 1) note:

> while decision researchers in a variety of fields, from cognitive psychology and neuroscience to behavioural economics, have increasingly studied and found evidence for the variety of ways in which affect influences people's choices, it is only rarely taken up in models of criminal decision making which are still dominated by cognitive approaches.

This goes some way to explaining why rational choice theory (RCT) has continued to be one of the most influential paradigms in criminology, despite its severely limited and 'sociologically hollow' (Hayward, 2007: 232) explanatory capacity.

Fallacies of rationality

It would be easy to limit theorizing about armed robbers to a consideration of their rational calculus, but, given the reality that most commercial armed robberies proceed in a manner that is chaotic and high risk and offers the likelihood of yielding only low rewards, the simplistic model has become inapposite for this crime type. Mainstream culture will continue to depict the archetypal robber as rational, intelligent, quick-witted, patient, and sophisticated; beguiling rogues who respect the art of armed robbery. A hold-up well executed is one in which no one gets hurt, the faceless bankers (the *real* criminals) are the only losers, and the police, although frustrated, acknowledge—even admire—the ingenuity, skill, and confidence demonstrated in the crime. For example, Danny Ocean, played by George Clooney in *Ocean's Eleven* (2001), a remake of the Rat Pack film *Ocean's 11* (1960), has three rules:

> Don't hurt anybody;
> Don't steal from anyone who doesn't deserve it; and
> Play the game like you've got nothing to lose.

The elaborate hold-ups depicted in films such as the *Ocean's* trilogy are a thing of fiction and far removed from the reality of most armed robberies—impulsive, chaotic, unpredictable, and ill thought-out. Frequently things do go wrong and people do get hurt—badly. Yet beyond the movie screen, scholarly studies have also portrayed armed robbers as largely rational actors pursuing substantial financial reward for relatively little time and effort (see Feeney, 1986; Gill, 2000; Morrison and O'Donnell, 1996). For example, Morrison and O'Donnell (1996: 183) assessed their 88 incarcerated interviewees as making 'logical calculations' on 'reasonably well-founded, balanced and accurate appraisal of the odds'.

In the current study, offenders who planned their offences beyond seizing a readily available weapon such as a kitchen or hunting knife and donning a rudimentary disguise, were in the minority, and they were typically committing their offences over a decade ago. One explanation is that offenders impose, consciously or not, a reconstructed 'fictional rationality' (Matthews, 2002: 38) on post hoc explanations of their offences. In reality they were more viscerally compelled, impulsive, and hectic. For the majority of participants in my study, the motives for and performance of robbery appeared to exist on the edge of reason, beyond rationality. Their reckless approach usually resulted in very small financial yields, thus inverting the risk–reward dichotomy.

A case for theoretical renewal: affective transgression

Criminology, as a discipline, is in need of theoretical renewal. In many ways the aetiological crises that ricocheted through its theoretical foundations have cleared the ground for a revitalized criminology that takes into account the liquidity of post-modernity, the revolutionary developments in technology that both facilitate and thwart criminal enterprise, and the corresponding transmutation in criminal modi operandi and expression. Built within any reconceptualizing of crime needs to be a recentring of the cultural embodiment and contextual aspects of offender behaviour. The administrative turn has marginalized much empirical research on the specific contexts of crime at precisely the time when criminal justice policy needs, more than ever before, to be grounded in detailed expert knowledge and data. A key aim of this book is to highlight the embodied and sensory experience of 'doing rob'. In doing so the concept of 'affective transgression' is proposed to account for the ways in which physiological, visceral, and emotional factors coalesce with the social and cultural expression of crime.

A trio of conceptual pillars scaffolds the concept of affective transgression—affect as *emotion*; affect as *transcendence*; and affect as *transformation*—to capture the complex motivations and performativity of armed robbers. The emotional and performative expression of criminal behaviour is highlighted, while its antecedence is located in culturally specific responses to prevailing social and economic structures. Applying this conceptualization to armed robbers throughout provides vital insights into the multiplicity of motivation beyond instrumental gain to expose the seductive appeal of robbery's emotional, transformational, and distinctive identity-building potential. In excavating multiple strands of affect, the analysis moves beyond 'affect-equals-emotions' theorizing to a more nuanced understanding of offender behaviour. Affective transgression expands the scope of criminological enquiry, inviting consideration of emotions, the body, and identity to help us to understand *why* it is that this crime is pursued and not others. The analysis provided in this book responds to the need to connect the visceral with the cultural, the somata with the social.

References

Anderson, C. (2016) 'Transnational histories of penal transportation: Punishment, labour and governance in the British imperial world, 1788–1939', *Australian Historical Studies* 47(3): 381–97.

Apter, M.J. (1992) *The Dangerous Edge: The Psychology of Excitement*. New York: Free Press.

Arlington, K. (2017) 'Record NSW prison population, rising assault rate, show a system "in a crisis"', *The Sydney Morning Herald*, 30 January.

Arnold, H. (2016) 'The prison officer' in: Y. Jewkes, J. Bennett, and B. Crewe (eds) *Handbook on Prisons* (2nd ed). Oxon: Routledge. 265–83.

Athens, L. (1989) *The Creation of Dangerous Violent Criminals*. London: Routledge.

Australian Bureau of Statistics (2019) 'Prisoners in Australia'. Available at: https://www.abs.gov.au/statistics/people/crime-and-justice/prisoners-australia/2019 (accessed: 24 June 2021).

Australian Government (n.d.) 'Convicts and the British colonies in Australia'. Available at: https://web.archive.org/web/20160101181100/http://www.australia.gov.au/about-australia/australian-story/convicts-and-the-british-colonies. Last updated 2014 (accessed: December 2019).

Australian Institute of Criminology (AIC) (2002) 'Service stations a target for robbery', *Crime Facts Info Series* No. 27. Canberra: Australian Institute of Criminology.

Australian Institute of Criminology (AIC) (2016) *Australian Crime: Facts and Figures 2014*. Canberra: Australian Institute of Criminology.

Australian Institute of Health and Welfare (2012) *The Mental Health of Prison Entrants in Australia 2010*. Bulletin no. 104, Cat. No. AUS 158. Canberra: AIHW.

Barthet, M., Fazekas G., and Sandler M. (2013) 'Music emotion recognition: From content- to context-based models' in: M. Aramaki, M. Barthet, R. Kronland-Martinet, and S. Ystad (eds) *From Sounds to Music and Emotions*. CMMR 2012. Lecture Notes in Computer Science, vol 7900. Berlin, Heidelberg: Springer, 228–52.

Bauman, Z. (1998) *Globalization: The Human Consequences*. New York: Columbia University Press.

Bauman, Z. (2013) *Liquid Times: Living in an Age of Uncertainty*. London: John Wiley & Sons.

Baumeister, R.F. (2001) *Evil: Inside Human Violence and Cruelty*. New York: Holt Paperbacks.

Baumeister, R.F. and Campbell, W.K. (1999) 'The intrinsic appeal of evil: Sadism, sensational thrills, and threatened egotism', *Personality and Social Psychology Review* 3(3): 210–21.

Beck, U. (1992) *Risk Society: Towards a New Modernity*. London: Sage.

Becker, G.S. (1968) 'Crime and punishment: An economic approach' in: N.G. Fielding, A. Clarke, and R. Witt (eds) *The Economic Dimensions of Crime*. London: Palgrave Macmillan, 13–68.

Begley, P. (2019) 'Parklea prison contract awarded to US company MTC despite "atrocious" record', *ABC News*, 27 November. Available at: https://www.abc.net.au/news/2019-11-28/sydney-prison-contract-awarded-to-controversial-company-mtc/11742766 (accessed: 21 June 2021).

Biles, D. (2012) 'The advantages of private prisons in Australia', *The Sydney Morning Herald*, 22 January. Available at: https://www.smh.com.au/politics/federal/the-advantages-of-private-prisons-in-australia-20120122-1te53.html (accessed: 11 January 2020).

Birkbeck, C. and LaFree, G. (1993) 'The situational analysis of crime and deviance', *Annual Review of Sociology* 19: 113–37.

Birmingham, L., Mason, D., and Grubin, D. (1999) 'The psychiatric implications of visible tattoos in an adult male prison population', *The Journal of Forensic Psychiatry* 10(3): 687–95.

Borzycki, M. (2003) 'Bank robbery in Australia', *Trends & Issues in Crime and Criminal Justice* no. 253. Available at: http://www.aic.gov.au/publications/tandi2/tandi253.html (accessed: 12 June 2021).

Borzycki, M. (2006) *Armed Robbery in Australia: 2004 National Armed Robbery Monitoring Program Annual Report*, Research and Public Policy Series No. 69. Canberra: Australian Institute of Criminology.

Borzycki, M. and Fuller, G. (2014) *Armed Robbery in Australia 2009–2010: National Armed Robbery Monitoring Program Report*. Monitoring Report no. 22. Canberra: Australian Institute of Criminology.

Bourdieu, P. (1998) *Acts of Resistance: Against the Tyranny of the Market* (trans. R. Nice). New York: Polity Press.

Braithwaite, J. (1989) *Crime, Shame and Reintegration*. Cambridge: Cambridge University Press.

Braithwaite, J. (1991) 'The criminal class and the making and breaking of Australia', *Australia and New Zealand Journal of Criminology* 24: 91–104.

Braithwaite, J. (1995) 'Diversion, reintegrative shaming and republican criminology' in: G. Albrecht and W. Ludwig-Mayerhofer (eds) *Diversion and Informal Social Control*. Berlin: Walter de Gruyter, 141–58.

Brook, B. (2017) 'Bed linen and boomerangs—the surprising products made by prisoners', News.com.au, 29 March. Available at: https://www.news.com.au/finance/business/other-industries/bed-linen-and-boomerangs-the-surprising-products-made-by-prisoners/news-story/d9cfbb0e9414fd00c0ef764ce8002982 (accessed: 21 June 2021).

Brown, J. (2014) *Anzac's Long Shadow*. Victoria, Australia: Redback.

Bushnell, A. (2017) *Australia's Criminal Justice Costs: An International Comparison*. Victoria, Australia: Institute of Public Affairs.

Byard, R. (2011) 'Ned Kelly tattoos: Origins and forensic implications', *Journal of Forensic and Legal Medicine* 18(6): 276–9.

Camus, A. (1951) *The Rebel* (Translation, 1953: Anthony Bower). London: Penguin Books.

Caulfield, L. and Hill, J. (2014) *Criminological Research for Beginners*. Oxon: Routledge.

Campbell, B. (1993) *Goliath: Britain's Dangerous Places*. London: Methuen.

Cisek, S.Z., Sedikides, C., Hart, C.M., Godwin, H.J., Benson, V., and Liversedge, S.P. (2014) 'Narcissism and consumer behaviour: A review and preliminary findings', *Frontiers in Psychology* 5(232): 1–9.

Cloward, R.A. and Ohlin, L.E. (1960) *Delinquency and Opportunity: A Study of Delinquent Gangs* (1st ed). London: Routledge.

Cohen, A.K. (1955) *Delinquent Boys: The Culture of the Gang*. New York: Free Press.

Cohen, S. (1972). *Folk Devils and Moral Panics*. London: MacGibbon and Kee.

Cohen, S. (2001) *States of Denial: Knowing about Atrocities and Suffering*. Cambridge: Polity Press.

Coleman, J. (1994) *The Criminal Elite: The Sociology of White Collar Crime*. New York: St. Martin's Press.

Collinson, D.L. (1988) 'Engineering humour: Masculinity, joking, and conflict in shop-floor relations', *Organization Studies* 9(2), 181–99.

Conversation, The (2017) 'FactCheck Q&A: are Indigenous Australians the most incarcerated people on Earth?' 6 June. Available at: www.theconversation.com (accessed: 6 September 2021).

Copes, H. and Hochstetler, A. (2010) 'Interviewing the incarcerated: Pitfalls and promises' in: W. Bernasco (ed) *Offenders on Offending: Learning about Crime from Criminals*. Devon: Willan Publishing, 49–67.

Cornish, D.B. and Clarke, R.V. (1986) *The Reasoning Criminal: Rational Choice Perspectives on Offending*. New York: Springer-Verlag.

Cousin, G. (2013) 'Reflexivity: The New Reflective Practice', *International Journal of Practice-based Learning in Health and Social Care* 1(2): 3–7.

Crawley, E. (2004) 'Emotion and performance: Prison officers and the presentation of self in prisons', *Punishment & Society* 6(4): 411–27.

Crime and Corruption Commission (2018) *Taskforce Flaxton: An Examination of Corruption Risks and Corruption in Queensland Prisons*. Brisbane, QLD: Crime and Corruption Commission.

Cromwell, P.F., Olson, J.N., and Avary, D.W. (1991) *Breaking and Entering: An Ethnographic Analysis of Burglary*. Los Angeles, CA: Sage.

Cromwell, P. and Thurman, Q. (2003) 'The devil made me do it: Use of neutralizations by shoplifters', *Deviant Behaviour* 24: 535–50.

Csikszentmihalyi, M. (1990) *Flow: The Psychology of Optimal Experience*. New York: Harper Perennial.

CSI NSW (2019) 'Welcome to Corrective Services Industries'. Available at: https://www.csi.nsw.gov.au/ (accessed: 11 January 2020).

Davis, M. (1995) 'Hell factories in the field: A prison-industrial complex', *The Nation*, 260(7): 229–34. Archive available at: http://archive.li/RF45D#selection-573.0-573.56 (accessed: 18 January 2020).

Davison, G. (1997) 'The great Australian sprawl', *Historic Environment* 13(1): 10–17.

Dean, R.A.K., and Gregory, D.M. (2005) 'More than trivial: Strategies for using humor in palliative care', *Cancer Nursing* 28(4): 292–300.

de Haan, W. and Loader, I. (2002) 'On the emotions of crime, punishment and social control', *Theoretical Criminology* 6(3): 243–53.

Donnelly, N. and Poynton, S. (2019) 'The effect of lockout and last drinks laws on non-domestic assaults in Sydney: An update to March 2019', NSW Bureau of Crime Statistics and Research No. 142. Available at: https://www.bocsar.nsw.gov.au/Documents/BB/2019-Report-Effect-of-lockout-and-last-drinks-laws-on-assaults-BB142.pdf (accessed: 6 January 2020).

Donoghue, J. and Tranter, B. (2014) 'The Anzac myth and Australian national identity'. Available at: http://www.bocsar.nsw.gov.au/Publications/BB/2019-Report-Effect-of-lockout-and-last-drinks-laws-on-assaults-BB142.pdf (accessed: 10 November 2021).

Dupréel, E. (1928) 'Le problème sociologique du rire', *Revue Philosophique* 106: 213–60.

Ellis, A., Winlow, S., and Hall, S. (2017) 'Throughout my life I've had people walk all over me': Trauma in the lives of violent men', *The Sociological Review* 65(4): 699–713.

Farrell, G., Tilley, N., Tseloni, A., and Mailley, J. (2008) 'The crime drop and the security hypothesis', *British Society of Criminology Newsletter* No. 62, Winter.

Farrell G, Tilley N, and Tseloni A. (2014) 'Why the crime drop?' *Crime and Justice* 43(1): 421–90.

Farrington, D.P., Coid, J.W., and Murray, J. (2009) 'Family factors in the intergenerational transmission of offending', *Criminal Behaviour and Mental Health* 19(2):109–24.

Feeney, F. (1986) 'Robbers as decision makers' in: D. Cornish and R. Clarke (eds) *The Reasoning Criminal*. New York: Springer-Verlag, 53–71.

Felson, R.B. and Massoglia, M. (2012) 'When is violence planned?' *Journal of Interpersonal Violence* 27(4): 753–74.

Ferrel, J. (2007) 'Cultural criminology' in G. Ritzer (ed) *Blackwell Encyclopedia of Sociology*. Oxford: Blackwell.

Folley, M. (2009) *Senna Versus Prost*. London: Penguin.

Forsyth, C.J., and Marckese, T.A. (1993) 'Thrills and skills: A sociological analysis of poaching', Deviant Behavior 14(2), 157–72.

Giddens, A. (2013) *Social Theory and Modern Sociology*. London: John Wiley & Sons.

Gill, M. (2000) *Commercial Robbery: Offenders' Perspectives on Security and Crime Prevention*. London: Blackstone Press.

Gilligan, J. (1996) *Violence: Reflections on a National Epidemic*. New York: Vintage.

Gilligan, J. (2000) *Violence: Reflections on our Deadliest Epidemic*. London: Kingsley.

Gowensmith, W.N. and Bloom, L.J. (1997) 'The effects of heavy metal music on arousal and anger', *Journal of Music Therapy* 34(1): 33–45.

Haebich, A. (2008) *Spinning the Dream: Assimilation in Australia 1950–1970*. North Freemantle, WA: Freemantle Press.

Haldane, R. (1995) *The People's Force: A History of the Victoria Police*. Carlton, Victoria: Melbourne University Press.

Halpern, D. (2005) *Social Capital*. Cambridge: Polity Press.

Hammerton, J. and Thomson, A. (2005) *Ten Pound Poms: Australia's Invisible Migrants*. Manchester, UK: Manchester University Press.

Harding, R. (1992) 'Private prisons in Australia', *Trends and Issues* No. 36. Canberra: Australian Institute of Criminology, 1–8.

Hayward, K. (2007) 'Situational crime prevention and its discontents: Rational choice theory versus the 'culture of now', *Social Policy & Administration* 41(3): 232–50.

Hayward, K. (2014) *City Limits:* Crime, Consumer Culture and the Urban Experience. London: The GlassHouse Press.

Hawkins, J. (2013) 'What better excuse for a real adventure': History, memory and tourism on the Kokoda Trail', *Public History Review* 20: 1–23.

Henning, K. and Holdford, R. (2006) 'Minimization, denial, and victim blaming by batterers: How much does the truth matter?' *Criminal Justice and Behavior* 33(1): 110–30.

Hepburn, A. (2003) *An Introduction to Critical Social Psychology*. London: Sage.

Hirschi, T. (1969) *Causes of Delinquency*. Berkeley, CA: University of California Press.

Hobbs, D. (1995) *Bad Business: Professional Crime in Modern Britain*. Oxford: Oxford University Press.

Hobbs, D. (2013) *Lush Life: Constructing Organized Crime in the UK*. Oxford: Oxford University Press.

Holmes, J. and Marra, M. (2002) 'Having a laugh at work: How humour contributes to workplace culture', *Journal of Pragmatics* 34: 1683–710.

Howells, K., Day, A., and Wright, S. (2004) 'Affect, emotions and sex offending', *Psychology, Crime and Law* 10(2): 179–95.

Hughes, R. (1987) *The Fatal Shore: The Epic of Australia's Founding*. New York: Alfred A. Knopf.

Jacobs, B.A. (2010) 'Serendipity in robbery selection', *British Journal of Criminology* 50: 514–29.

Jackson-Jacobs, C. (2013) 'Constructing physical fights: An interactionist analysis of violence among affluent, suburban youth', *Qualitative Sociology* 36: 23–52.

Jacques, S. and Wright, R. (2010) 'Apprehending criminals: The impact of law on offender-based research' in: W. Bernasco (ed) *Offenders on Offending: Learning about crime from criminals*. Devon: Willan Publishing, 23–45.

Jewkes, Y. (2011) 'Autoethnography and emotion as intellectual resources: Doing prison research differently', *Qualitative Inquiry* 18: 63–75.

Katz, J. (1988) Seductions *of Crime; Moral and Sensual Attractions in Doing Evil*. New York: Basic Books.

Katz, J. (1999) *How Emotions Work*. Chicago, IL and London: University of Chicago Press.

Kemp, M. (2011) 'Why a Ned Kelly tattoo is dangerous', *The Advertiser*, 17 June 2011. Available at: https://www.adelaidenow.com.au/news/why-a-ned-kelly-tattoo-is-dangerous/news-story/cc0ff2abb1c63f50c7c6a978d0fb390b (accessed: 30 January 2020).

Kennedy, J.J. (1988) *Commission of Review into Corrective Services in Queensland.* Queensland: Queensland Corrective Services.

Kilby, J. and Ray, L. (2014) 'Introduction' in J. Kilby and L. Ray (eds) *Violence and Society: Toward a New Sociology*. Chichester: John Wiley and Sons, 1–12.

Klockars, C.B. (1974) *The Professional Fence*. New York: Free Press.

Kuhlman, T. (1988) 'Gallows humor for a scaffold setting: Managing aggressive patients in a maximum security forensic unit', *Hospital and Community Psychiatry* 39(10): 1085–90.

Lambe, S., Hamilton-Giachritsis, C., Garner, E., and Walker, J. (2018) 'The role of narcissism in aggression and violence: A systematic review', *Trauma, Violence & Abuse* 19(2): 209–30.

Larkin, R.W. (1979) *Suburban Youth in Cultural Crisis*. New York: Oxford University Press.

Lasch, C. (1979) *The Culture of Narcissism: American Life in an Age of Diminishing Expectations*. New York: Norton.

Laws, B. and Crewe, B. (2016) 'Emotion regulation among male prisoners', *Theoretical Criminology* 20(4): 529–47.

Lee, D. (2013) 'Days of the "bank job" are numbered report suggests', *BBC News*, 27 December. Available at: https://www.bbc.co.uk/news/technology-25526671 (accessed: 18 June 2021).

Leith, K.P. and Baumeister, R.F. (1996) 'Why do bad moods increase self-defeating behavior? Emotion, risk taking, and self-regulation', *Journal of Personality and Social Psychology* 17(6): 1250–67.

Luckenbill, D.F. (1977) 'Criminal homicide as a situated transaction', *Social Problems* 25: 176–86.

Luckenbill, D.F. (1981) 'Generating compliance: The case of robbery', *Urban Life* 10: 25–46.

Lumsden, K. and Winter, A. (2014) 'Reflexivity in criminological research' in K. Lumsden and A. Winter (eds) *Reflexivity in Criminological Research: Experiences with the Powerful and the Powerless*. Basingstoke: Palgrave Macmillan, 1–20.

Lyng, S. (1990) 'Edgework: A Social Psychological Analysis of Voluntary Risk Taking', *The American Journal of Sociology* 95(4): 851-886.

Lyng, S. (2004) *Edgework: The Sociology of Risk-Taking*. New York: Routledge.

Macquarie Dictionary (2012) 'The Aussie battler', Macquarie Dictionary. Available at: https://www.macquariedictionary.com.au/blog/article/104/ (accessed: 24 February 2020).

MailOnline (2011) 'Are you sure you want a Ned Kelly tattoo? Australians inked with outlaw "more likely to meet a violent death"', 17 June. Available at: https://www.dailymail.co.uk/news/article-2004414/Australians-inked-Ned-Kelly-tattoo-likely-meet-violent-death.html (accessed: 30 January 2020).

Marlborough, P. (2018) 'Waltzing Matilda is Australia's creepiest ballad. Let me tell you why', *The Guardian*, 31 October. Available at: https://www.theguardian.com/music/2018/oct/31/waltzing-matilda-is-australias-creepiest-ballad-let-me-tell-you-why (accessed: 15 December 2019).

Maruna, S and Copes, H. (2005) 'What have we learned from five decades of neutralization research?', *Crime and Justice* 32: 221–320.

Massumi, B. (2015) *Politics of Affect*. Cambridge: Polity Press.

Matthews, R. (2002) *Armed Robbery*. Cullompton: Willan Publishing.

Matthews, R. (2016) 'Realist criminology, the new aetiological crisis and the crime drop', *International Journal for Crime, Justice and Social Democracy* 5(3): 2–11.

Matza, D. (1964) *Delinquency and Drift*. New York: Wiley.

Matza, D. (1969) *Becoming Deviant*. New Jersey, USA: Prentice-Hall.

McCord, J. (1991) 'The cycle of crime and socialization practices', *Journal of Criminal Law and Criminology* 82(1): 211–28.

Meyer, W.M. (2011) 'Beyond the seas: Eighteenth-century convict transportation and the widening net of penal sanctions'. Unpublished dissertation. University of California, Berkeley.

Minor, W.W. (1981) 'Techniques of neutralization: A reconceptualization and empirical examination', *Journal of Research in Crime and Delinquency* 18(2): 295–318.

Molony, J. (2001) *Ned Kelly*. Victoria, Australia: Melbourne University Publishing.

Morrison, S. and O'Donnell, I. (1996) 'An analysis of the decision making practices of armed robbers' in: R. Homel (ed) *The Politics and Practice of Situational Crime Prevention*. Monsey, NY: Criminal Justice Press, 159–88.

Mouzos, J. and Borzycki, M. (2003) 'An exploratory analysis of armed robbery in Australia', Technical and Background Paper Series, no. 7. Canberra: Australian Institute of Criminology.

Mouzos, J. and Rushforth, C. (2003) 'Firearm related deaths in Australia 1991–2001', *Trends & Issues in Crime and Criminal Justice* no. 269, 1–6.

Mullins, C. (2006) *Holding Your Square: Masculinities, Streetlife and Violence*. Cullompton: Willan Publishing.

Nalla, M.K. and Wakefield, A. (2014) 'The security officer' in: M. Gill (ed) *The Handbook of Security*. Basingstoke: Palgrave Macmillan, 727–46.

Nassauer, A. (2018) 'How robberies succeed or fail: Analyzing crime caught on CCTV', *Journal of Research in Crime and Delinquency* 55(1) 125–54.

Nayak, A. (2006) 'Displaced masculinities: Chavs, youth and class in the post-industrial city', *Sociology* 40(5): 813–31.

Nee, C. (2003) 'Research on burglary at the end of the millennium: A grounded approach to understanding crime', *Security Journal* 16: 37–44.

Nee, C. and Meenaghan, A. (2006) 'Expert decision making in burglars', *British Journal of Criminology* 46: 935–49.

Nee, C. and Taylor, M. (2000) 'Examining burglars' target selection: Interview, experiment, or ethnomethodology?' *Psychology, Crime and Law* 6, 45–59.

Nielsen, M.M. (2011) 'On humour in prison', *European Journal of Criminology* 8(6): 500–14.

Nolan, K. and Anyon, J. (2004) 'Learning to do time: Willis' cultural reproduction model in an era of deindustrialization, globalization, and the mass incarceration of people of color' in: N. Dolby, G. Dimitriadis, and P. Willis (eds) *Learning to Labor in New Times*. New York: Routledge, 114–29.

NSW Government (2018) 'Fact Sheet 7: Corrective services industries'. Available at: https://www.correctiveservices.justice.nsw.gov.au/Documents/CSNSW%20Fact%20Sheets/corrective-services-industries.pdf (accessed: 30 January 2020).

NSW Legislative Council (2018) *Parklea Correctional Centre and other operational issues*. Portfolio Committee No. 4—Legal Affairs. Available at: https://www.parliament.nsw.gov.au/lcdocs/inquiries/2470/Report%20No%2038%20-%20Parklea%20Correctional%20Centre%20and%20other%20operational%20issues.pdf (accessed: 12 January 2020).

O'Donnell, I. and Morrison, S. (1997) 'Armed and dangerous? The use of firearms in robbery', *The Howard Journal* 36(3): 305–20.

O'Malley, P. and Mugford, S. (1994) 'Crime, excitement and modernity' in G. Barak (ed) *Varieties of Criminology*. Westport, CT: Praeger, 188–210.

O'Reilly, N. (2012) *Exploring Suburbia: The Suburbs in the Contemporary Australian Novel*. Amherst, NY: Teneo Press.

Orwell, G. (1944) 'Benefit of clergy: Some notes on Salvador Dali', The Saturday Book for 1944. Available at: https://orwell.ru/library/reviews/dali/english/e_dali (accessed: 3 May 2021).

Oxford Australia (2015) 'Word of the month: Ned Kelly Beard'. Available at: http://lib.oup.com.au/general/Dictionaries/WOTM/2015/WOTM_March_2015.pdf (accessed 15 December 2019).

Palmer, D. (2003) 'A new police in Victoria: Conditions of crises or politics of reform? 150 Years of the Victoria Police', *Victorian Historical Journal* 74(2): 167–96.

Petersilia, J., Greenwood, P., and Lavin, M. (1978) *Criminal Careers of Habitual Felons*. Washington, DC: US Department of Justice.

Petrosino, A. and Brensibler, D. (2003) 'The motives, methods and decision making of convenience store robbers: Interviews with 28 incarcerated offenders in Massachusetts' in: M. Smith and D. Cornish (eds) *Theory for Practice in Situational Crime Prevention Studies*, vol 16. New York: Criminal Justice Press, 237–64.

Pfefferbaum, B. and Wood, P.B. (1994) 'Self report study of impulsive and delinquent behaviour in college students', *Journal of Adolescent Health* 15: 295–302.

Philips, K. (2017) 'Thousands of immigrants detained by America claim they were forced into labour, a violation of anti-slavery laws', *The Independent*, 5 March 2017. Available at: https://www.independent.co.uk/news/world/americas/us-politics/thousands-of-immigrants-detained-by-america-claim-they-were-forced-into-labour-a-violation-of-anti-a7612636.html (accessed: 19 January 2020).

Pogrebin, M.R. and Poole, E.D. (1988) 'Humour in the briefing room: A study of the strategic uses of humor among police', *Journal of Contemporary Ethnography* 17(2): 183–210.

Pole, C. and Lampard, R. (2002) *Practical Social Investigation: Qualitative and Quantitative Methods in Social Research*. Harlow: Prentice Hall.

Presdee, M. (2000) *Cultural Criminology and the Carnival of Crime*. Routledge: Oxon.

Presdee, M. (2004) 'Cultural criminology: The long and winding road', *Theoretical Criminology* 8(3): 275–85.

Productivity Commission (2019) Report on Government Services 2019. Available at: https://www.pc.gov.au/research/ongoing/report-on-government-services/2019/justice/corrective-services (accessed: 4 November 2021).

Productivity Commission (2020) Report on Government Services 2020. Available at: https://www.pc.gov.au/research/ongoing/report-on-government-services/2020/justice/corrective-services (accessed: 5 July 2021).

Raine, A. (2013) *The Anatomy of Violence: The Biological Roots of Crime*. New York: Vintage Books.

Rogerson-Revell, P. (2007) 'Humour in business: A double-edged sword: A study of humour and style shifting in intercultural business meetings', *Journal of Pragmatics* 39(1): 4–28.

Rowe, D.C. and Farrington, D.P. (1997) 'The Familial Transmission of Criminal Convictions', *Criminology* 35(1): 177–202.

Rowse, T. and A. Moran (1984) '"Peculiarly Australian": The political construction of cultural identity' in: S. Encel and L. Bryson (eds) *Australian Society*. Sydney: Longman Cheshire, 229–47.

Rubin, A.T. (2012) 'The unintended consequences of penal reform: A case study of penal transportation in eighteenth-century London', *Law & Society Review* 46(4): 815–51.

Rudd, K. (2010) Anzac Day 2010: National Ceremony commemorative address. Available at: https://www.awm.gov.au/commemoration/speeches/national-ceremony-commemorative-address-2010 (accessed: 8 November 2021).

Sands, V., O'Neill, D., and Hodge, G. (2019) 'Cheaper, better, and more accountable? Twenty-five years of prisons privatisation in Victoria', *Australian Journal of Public Administration* 78: 577–95.

Savage, J. (2018) 'Demonising those teenage dirtbags: The current moral outcry over drill music is so last century. Adults have been scared about what the kids are singing for decades', *Index on Censorship* 47(2), 66–9.

Scheff, T. and Retzinger, S.M. (1991) *Emotions and Violence: Shame and Rage in Destructive Conflicts*. San Francisco, CA: Jossey Bass Wiley.

Schlosser, E. (1998) 'The Prison-Industrial Complex', *The Atlantic*, December. Available at: https://www.theatlantic.com/magazine/archive/1998/12/the-prison-industrial-complex/304669/ (accessed: 21 June 2021).

Scott, T. (2007). Expression of humour by emergency personnel involved with sudden deathwork. *Mortality* 12(4), 350–64.

Scott, R. and MacFarlane, I. (2014) 'Ned Kelly—stock thief, bank robber, murderer—psychopath', Psychiatry, Psychology and Law 21(5): 716–46.

Sedgwick, E.K. (2003) *Touching Feeling: Affect, Pedagogy, Performativity*. Durham, NC: Duke University Press.

Seigworth, G.J. and Gregg, M. (2010) 'An inventory of shimmers' in: M. Gregg and G.J. Seigworth (eds) The Affect Theory Reader. Durham, NC: Duke University Press, 1–28.

Selfhout, M.H., Delsing, M.J., ter Bogt, T.F., and Meeus, W.H. (2008) 'Heavy metal and hip-hop style preferences and externalizing problem behavior: A two-wave longitudinal study', *Youth & Society* 39(4): 435–52.

Shammas, V.L. (2017) 'Pains of imprisonment' in: K.R. Kerley (ed) *The Encyclopedia of Corrections*. Wiley Online Library.

Simon, H.A. (1990) 'Bounded rationality' in: J. Eatwell, M. Milgate, and P. Newman (eds) Utility and Probability. London: Palgrave Macmillan, 15–8.

Spinoza, B. (1994). *Ethics*, trans. by E. Curley in: *A Spinoza Reader.* New Jersey: Princeton University Press.

Sudbury, J. (2004) 'A world without prisons: Resisting militarism, globalized punishment, and empire', *Social Justice* 31(1–2): 9–30.

Sutherland, E. (1947) *Principles of Criminology* (4th ed). Philadelphia, PA: Lippincott.

Sutherland, E. and Cressey, D. (1970) *Principles of Criminology* (8th ed). Philadelphia, PA: Lippincott.

Swanson, R. (1986). 'Convenience store robbery analysis: A research study of robbers, victims, and environment. Gainesville, FL' in: W.J. Clifton (ed.) *Convenience Robberies: An Intervention Strategy by the Gainesville Police Department.* Gainesville, FL: Gainesville Police Department.

Sykes, G. and Matza, D. (1957) 'Techniques of neutralization, a theory of delinquency', *American Sociological Review* 22(6): 664–70.

Tavan, G. (2005) *The Long, Slow Death of White Australia.* Carlton North, Victoria: Scribe Publications.

Taylor, E. (2014) 'Honour among thieves? Exploring the morality and rationality of convicted domestic burglars', Criminology and Criminal Justice; An International Journal 14(4): 487–502.

Taylor, E. (2017a) '"I should have been a security consultant": The Good Lives Model and residential burglars', *European Journal of Criminology* 14(4): 434–50.

Taylor, E. (2017b) 'On the edge of reason? Armed robbery, affective transgression, and bounded rationality', *Deviant Behavior* 38(8): 928–40.

Taylor, E. (2019) *It's Not Part of the Job: Violence and Verbal Abuse Toward Shop Workers.* Manchester, UK: The Co-op.

Taylor, L. (1985) *In the Underworld.* London: Allen & Unwin.

Thrift, N. (2004) 'Intensities of feeling: Towards a spatial politics of affect', *Geografiska Annaler* 86B(1): 57–78.

Tomkins, S. (1962) *Affect Imagery Consciousness.* New York: Springer.

Tomkins, S. (2008) *Affect Imagery Consciousness: The Complete Edition: Two Volumes.* New York: Springer.

Topalli, V. and Wright, R. (2013) 'Affect and the dynamic foreground of predatory street crime' in: J.L. van Gelder, H. Elffers, D. Reynald, and D. Nagin (eds) *Affect and Cognition in Criminal Decision Making.* London: Routledge, 42–57.

Turnbull, C. (1942) *Ned Kelly: Being His Own Story of His Life and Crimes.* Melbourne, Australia: Hawthorn Press.

United Nations Office on Drugs and Crime (2008) *Monitoring the Impact of Economic Crisis on Crime.* Vienna: UNODC Statistics and Surveys Section.

van Gelder, J.L., Elffers, H., Reynald, D., and Nagin, D. (2014) 'Affect and cognition in criminal decision making: Between rational choices and lapses of self-control' in: J.L. van Gelder, H. Elffers, D. Reynald, and D. Nagin (eds) *Affect and Cognition in Criminal Decision Making.* London: Routledge, 1–19.

Veblen, T. (1899) *The Theory of the Leisure Class*: An Economic Study of Institutions. New York: B.W. Huebsch.

Walker, J. and Bright, J. (2009) 'False inflated self-esteem and violence: A systematic review and cognitive model', *Journal of Forensic Psychiatry & Psychology* 20: 1–32.

Walsh, D. (1986). *Heavy Business: Commercial Burglary and Robbery*. London: Routledge.

Wellford, C.F., MacDonald, J., and Weiss, J.C. (1997). *Multistate Study of Convenience Store Robberies*. Washington, DC: Justice Research and Statistics Association. Available at: https://www.ncjrs.gov/pdffiles1/nij/grants/173772.pdf (accessed: 10 January 2020).

Wetherell, M. (2012) *Affect and Emotion: A New Social Science Understanding*. London: Sage.

White, R. (1979) 'The Australian way of life', *Historical Studies* 18(73): 528–45.

Wilkie, K. (2018) 'Qantas capitalises on prison labour as it's revealed jailbirds being paid less than the minimum wage are taking jobs from the private sector', *MailOnline*. 24 October. Available at: https://www.dailymail.co.uk/news/article-6309849/Qantas-capitalises-prison-labour-revealed-jailbirds-paid-minimum-wage.html (accessed: 24 October 2018).

Williams, M. (2015) 'Stain or badge of honour? Convict heritage inspires mixed feelings', *The Conversation*, 8 June. Available at: https://theconversation.com/stain-or-badge-of-honour-convict-heritage-inspires-mixed-feelings-41097 (accessed: 6 September 2021).

Willis, P. (1977) *Learning to Labour: How Working Class Kids Get Working Class Jobs*. Farnborough: Saxon House.

World Prison Brief (2019) 'Highest to lowest—Prison population rate'. Institute for Crime and Justice Policy Research. Available at: https://www.prisonstudies.org/highest-to-lowest/prison_population_rate?field_region_taxonomy_tid=All (accessed: 15 January 2020).

Wright, R.T. and Bennett, T. (1990) 'Exploring the offender's perspective: Observing and interviewing criminals', *Measurement Issues in Criminology* New York, NY: Springer-Verlag, 138–51.

Wright, R.T. and Decker, S.H. (1994) *Burglars on the Job: Streetlife and Residential Break-ins*. Boston, MA: Northeastern University Press.

Wright, R.T. and Decker, S.H. (1997) *Armed Robbers in Action: Stick ups and Street Culture*. Boston, MA: Northeastern University Press.

Wright, R.T., Brookman, F., and Bennett, T. (2006) 'The foreground dynamics of street robbery in Britain', *British Journal of Criminology* 46(1): 1–15.

Wright, J.D. and Rossi, P.H. (1986) *Armed and Considered Dangerous: A Survey of Felons and Their Firearms*. New York: Aldine de Gruyter.

Yar, M. (2009) 'Neither scylla nor charybdis: Overcoming the dualism between reason and the emotions in criminology', *Internet Journal of Criminology*, Available at: https://958be75a-da42-4a45-aafa-549955018b18.filesusr.com/ugd/b93dd4_1917a53e0d2448de8de9348856156beb.pdf (accessed: 10 November 2021).

Young, J. (1994) *The Exclusive Society: Social Exclusion, Crime and Difference in Late Modernity*. London and Thousand Oaks, CA: Sage Publications.

Young, J. (1997) 'Left realist criminology: Radical in its analysis, realist in its policy' in: M. Maguire, R. Morgan, and R. Reiner (eds) *Oxford Handbook of Criminology* (2nd ed). Oxford: Oxford University Press, 473–97.

Young, J. (2003) 'Merton with energy, Katz with structure: The sociology of vindictiveness and the criminology of transgression', *Theoretical Criminology* 7(3): 389–414.
Young, J. (2004) 'Voodoo criminology and the numbers game' in: K. Hayward, W. Morrison, and M. Presdee (eds) *Cultural Criminology Unleashed*. London: Glasshouse Press, 13–28.
Young, J. (2007) *The Vertigo of Late Modernity*. London: Sage.
Zournazi, M. (2003) *Hope: New Philosophies for Change*. Routledge: New York.

Index

For the benefit of digital users, indexed terms that span two pages (e.g., 52–53) may, on occasion, appear on only one of those pages.